D1482991

THE
INNU
(THE MONTAGNAIS-NASKAPI)

THE
INNU

(THE MONTAGNAIS-NASKAPI)

Peter Armitage
Memorial University of Newfoundland

Frank W. Porter III
General Editor

CHELSEA HOUSE PUBLISHERS
New York   Philadelphia

On the cover A ceremonial robe of tanned unsmoked caribou skin. The geometric patterns in the center were painted by the wife of Old Sam, a shaman from the Davis Inlet Innu.

Chelsea House Publishers
Editor-in-Chief Remmel Nunn
Managing Editor Karyn Gullen Browne
Copy Chief Juliann Barbato
Picture Editor Adrian G. Allen
Art Director Maria Epes
Deputy Copy Chief Mark Rifkin
Assistant Art Director Loraine Machlin
Manufacturing Manager Gerald Levine
Systems Manager Rachel Vigier
Production Manager Joseph Romano
Production Coordinator Marie Claire Cebrián

Indians of North America
Senior Editor Liz Sonneborn

Staff for **THE INNU**
Assistant Editor Claire Wilson
Copy Editor Philip Koslow
Editorial Assistant Nicole Claro
Designer Donna Sinisgalli
Assistant Designer James Baker
Picture Researcher Alan Gottlieb

First Printing

1 3 5 7 9 8 6 4 2

Library of Congress Cataloging-in-Publication Data

Armitage, Peter.
The Innu (Montagnais-Naskapi)/by Peter Armitage.
p. cm.—(Indians of North America)
Includes bibliographical references.
Summary: Examines the history, culture, changing fortunes, and future prospects of the Innu (Montagnais-Naskapi) Indians. Includes a picture essay on their crafts.
ISBN 1-55546-717-2
0-7910-0389-2 (pbk.)
1. Montagnais Indians. 2. Nascapee Indians. [1. Montagnais Indians. 2. Nascapee Indians. 3. Indians of North America.]
I. Title II. Series: Indians of North America
(Chelsea House Publishers)
E99.M87A66 1990
971'.004973—dc20

89-13924
CIP
AC

CONTENTS

INDIANS OF NORTH AMERICA

CHELSEA HOUSE PUBLISHERS

INDIANS OF NORTH AMERICA: CONFLICT AND SURVIVAL

Frank W. Porter III

The Indians survived our open intention of wiping them out, and since the tide turned they have even weathered our good intentions toward them, which can be much more deadly.

John Steinbeck
America and Americans

When Europeans first reached the North American continent, they found hundreds of tribes occupying a vast and rich country. The newcomers quickly recognized the wealth of natural resources. They were not, however, so quick or willing to recognize the spiritual, cultural, and intellectual riches of the people they called Indians.

The Indians of North America examines the problems that develop when people with different cultures come together. For American Indians, the consequences of their interaction with non-Indian people have been both productive and tragic. The Europeans believed they had "discovered" a "New World," but their religious bigotry, cultural bias, and materialistic world view kept them from appreciating and understanding the people who lived in it. All too often they attempted to change the way of life of the indigenous people. The Spanish conquistadores wanted the Indians as a source of labor. The Christian missionaries, many of whom were English, viewed them as potential converts. French traders and trappers used the Indians as a means to obtain pelts. As Francis Parkman, the 19th-century historian, stated, "Spanish civilization crushed the Indian; English civilization scorned and neglected him; French civilization embraced and cherished him."

Nearly 500 years later, many people think of American Indians as curious vestiges of a distant past, waging a futile war to survive in a Space Age society. Even today, our understanding of the history and culture of American Indians is too often derived from unsympathetic, culturally biased, and inaccurate reports. The American Indian, described and portrayed in thousands of movies, television programs, books, articles, and government studies, has either been raised to the status of the "noble savage" or disparaged as the "wild Indian" who resisted the westward expansion of the American frontier.

Where in this popular view are the real Indians, the human beings and communities whose ancestors can be traced back to ice-age hunters? Where are the creative and indomitable people whose sophisticated technologies used the natural resources to ensure their survival, whose military skill might even have prevented European settlement of North America if not for devastating epidemics and disruption of the ecology? Where are the men and women who are today diligently struggling to assert their legal rights and express once again the value of their heritage?

The various Indian tribes of North America, like people everywhere, have a history that includes population expansion, adaptation to a range of regional environments, trade across wide networks, internal strife, and warfare. This was the reality. Europeans justified their conquests, however, by creating a mythical image of the New World and its native people. In this myth, the New World was a virgin land, waiting for the Europeans. The arrival of Christopher Columbus ended a timeless primitiveness for the original inhabitants.

Also part of this myth was the debate over the origins of the American Indians. Fantastic and diverse answers were proposed by the early explorers, missionairies, and settlers. Some thought that the Indians were descended from the Ten Lost Tribes of Israel, others that they were descended from inhabitants of the lost continent of Atlantis. One writer suggested that the Indians had reached North America in another Noah's ark.

A later myth, perpetrated by many historians, focused on the relentless persecution during the past five centuries until only a scattering of these "primitive" people remained to be herded onto reservations. This view fails to chronicle the overt and covert ways in which the Indians successfully coped with the intruders.

All of these myths presented one-sided interpretations that ignored the complexity of European and American events and policies. All left serious questions unanswered. What were the origins of the American Indians? Where did they come from? How and when did they get to the New World? What was their life—their culture—really like?

In the late 1800s, anthropologists and archaeologists in the Smithsonian Institution's newly created Bureau of American Ethnology in Washington,

D.C., began to study scientifically the history and culture of the Indians of North America. They were motivated by an honest belief that the Indians were on the verge of extinction and that along with them would vanish their languages, religious beliefs, technology, myths, and legends. These men and women went out to visit, study, and record data from as many Indian communities as possible before this information was forever lost.

By this time there was a new myth in the national consciousness. American Indians existed as figures in the American past. They had performed a historical mission. They had challenged white settlers who trekked across the continent. Once conquered, however, they were supposed to accept graciously the way of life of their conquerors.

The reality again was different. American Indians resisted both actively and passively. They refused to lose their unique identity, to be assimilated into white society. Many whites viewed the Indians not only as members of a conquered nation but also as "inferior" and "unequal." The rights of the Indians could be expanded, contracted, or modified as the conquerors saw fit. In every generation, white society asked itself what to do with the American Indians. Their answers have resulted in the twists and turns of federal Indian policy.

There were two general approaches. One way was to raise the Indians to a "higher level" by "civilizing" them. Zealous missionaries considered it their Christian duty to elevate the Indian through conversion and scanty education. The other approach was to ignore the Indians until they disappeared under pressure from the ever-expanding white society. The myth of the "vanishing Indian" gave stronger support to the latter option, helping to justify the taking of the Indians' land.

Prior to the end of the 18th century, there was no national policy on Indians simply because the American nation has not yet come into existence. American Indians similarly did not possess a political or social unity with which to confront the various Europeans. They were not homogeneous. Rather, they were loosely formed bands and tribes, speaking nearly 300 languages and thousands of dialects. The collective identity felt by Indians today is a result of their common experiences of defeat and/or mistreatment at the hands of whites.

During the colonial period, the British crown did not have a coordinated policy toward the Indians of North America. Specific tribes (most notably the Iroquois and the Cherokee) became military and political pawns used by both the crown and the individual colonies. The success of the American Revolution brought no immediate change. When the United States acquired new territory from France and Mexico in the early 19th century, the federal government wanted to open this land to settlement by homesteaders. But the Indian tribes that lived on this land had signed treaties with European governments assuring their title to the land. Now the United States assumed legal responsibility for honoring these treaties.

At first, President Thomas Jefferson believed that the Louisiana Purchase contained sufficient land for both the Indians and the white population. Within a generation, though, it became clear that the Indians would not be allowed to remain. In the 1830s the federal government began to coerce the eastern tribes to sign treaties agreeing to relinquish their ancestral land and move west of the Mississippi River. Whenever these negotiations failed, President Andrew Jackson used the military to remove the Indians. The southeastern tribes, promised food and transportation during their removal to the West, were instead forced to walk the "Trail of Tears." More than 4,000 men, woman, and children died during this forced march. The "removal policy" was successful in opening the land to homesteaders, but it created enormous hardships for the Indians.

By 1871 most of the tribes in the United States had signed treaties ceding most or all of their ancestral land in exchange for reservations and welfare. The treaty terms were intended to bind both parties for all time. But in the General Allotment Act of 1887, the federal government changed its policy again. Now the goal was to make tribal members into individual landowners and farmers, encouraging their absorption into white society. This policy was advantageous to whites who were eager to acquire Indian land, but it proved disastrous for the Indians. One hundred thirty-eight million acres of reservation land were subdivided into tracts of 160, 80, or as little as 40 acres, and allotted tribe members on an individual basis. Land owned in this way was said to have "trust status" and could not be sold. But the surplus land—all Indian land not allotted to individuals—was opened (for sale) to white settlers. Ultimately, more than 90 million acres of land were taken from the Indians by legal and illegal means.

The resulting loss of land was a catastrophe for the Indians. It was necessary to make it illegal for Indians to sell their land to non-Indians. The Indian Reorganization Act of 1934 officially ended the allotment period. Tribes that voted to accept the provisions of this act were reorganized, and an effort was made to purchase land within preexisting reservations to restore an adequate land base.

Ten years later, in 1944, federal Indian policy again shifted. Now the federal government wanted to get out of the "Indian business." In 1953 an act of Congress named specific tribes whose trust status was to be ended "at the earliest possible time." This new law enabled the United States to end unilaterally, whether the Indians wished it or not, the special status that protected the land in Indian tribal reservations. In the 1950s federal Indian policy was to transfer federal responsibility and jurisdiction to state governments, encourage the physical relocation of Indian peoples from reservations to urban areas, and hasten the termination, or extinction, of tribes.

Between 1954 and 1962 Congress passed specific laws authorizing the termination of more than 100 tribal groups. The stated purpose of the termination policy was to ensure the full and complete integration of Indians into American society. However, there is a less benign way to interpret this legislation. Even as termination was being discussed in Congress, 133 separate bills were introduced to permit the transfer of trust land ownership from Indians to non-Indians.

With the Johnson administration in the 1960s the federal government began to reject termination. In the 1970s yet another Indian policy emerged. Known as "self-determination," it favored keeping the protective role of the federal government while increasing tribal participation in, and control of, important areas of local government. In 1983 President Reagan, in a policy statement on Indian affairs, restated the unique "government is government" relationship of the United States with the Indians. However, federal programs since then have moved toward transferring Indian affairs to individual states, which have long desired to gain control of Indian land and resources.

As long as American Indians retain power, land, and resources that are coveted by the states and the federal government, there will continue to be a "clash of cultures," and the issues will be contested in the courts, Congress, the White House, and even in the international human rights community. To give all Americans a greater comprehension of the issues and conflicts involving American Indians today is a major goal of this series. These issues are not easily understood, nor can these conflicts be readily resolved. The study of North American Indian history and culture is a necessary and important step toward that comprehension. All Americans must learn the history of the relations between the Indians and the federal government, recognize the unique legal status of the Indians, and understand the heritage and cultures of the Indians of North America.

A somewhat romanticized 1612 engraving of an Innu family.

PREHISTORIC
COLONISTS

Long ago, Kuekuatsheu, the wolverine, built a big boat and put animals from all species inside it. It then began to rain heavily, and the land became flooded. Kuekuatsheu told the mink to dive into the water to retrieve some mud and rocks, which the wolverine mixed together to make an island. This island became the world that all humans and other animals inhabit today.

This is the story of how the world was created, according to the Innu people of northeastern Canada. Before Europeans arrived in North America, these Indians inhabited the Quebec-Labrador peninsula, which includes portions of what are now the provinces of Quebec and Newfoundland. They called their territory Nitassinan, literally "our land," a name they continue to use today. The Innu now number approximately 10,000, the majority of whom live in the Province of Quebec, in the communities of St. Augustin, La Ro-

maine, Natashquan, Mingan, Sept-Îles, Maliotenam, Schefferville, Kawawachi-kamach, Betsiamites, Pointe-Bleue, and Les Escoumins. The remainder inhabit the communities of Sheshatshit and Davis Inlet in Labrador.

Until recently, non-Indians have referred to the Innu as Montagnais-Naskapi. The term *Montagnais* was first used by the French explorer and settler Samuel de Champlain, who encountered Innu people at the mouth of the Saguenay River in the early 1600s. He called them Montagnais because of the high mountains (*montagnes* in French) in their territory. According to anthropologist José Mailhot, Europeans later referred to other Indian groups that they contacted in the interior of the Quebec-Labrador peninsula as Montagnais. However, by the early 19th century, Europeans used the term to describe only those Innu that they considered more "civilized" than others in

13

the area. These "Montagnais" tended to live closer to the Gulf of St. Lawrence in the southern part of the peninsula, and most of them had been baptized.

The term *Naskapi* has a more complicated origin. Mailhot says it was originally "borrowed" by the French from the Saguenay River Innu during the 17th century. In the Innu language, the word meant "people of the place where it fades from sight" and referred to groups that lived beyond the horizon. In 1643, the term first appeared in the records of Catholic missionaries in North America as *Ounachkapiouek*; it was not until 1733 that *Naskapi* appeared in its modern form.

At first Europeans used the term *Naskapi* to describe just a particular group of Innu. But later the word took on a negative meaning. It was used by missionaries to refer to the Innu people they considered the most primitive. These were generally groups that had maintained their traditional religion. Later, in the mid-19th century, the Canadian government used the term to refer to Indians who were not subject to its jurisdiction and did not live in year-round settlements. By the late 19th century, Euro-Canadians generally referred to Innu living farthest away from trading posts and missions in the northeastern portions of the Quebec-Labrador peninsula as Naskapi.

More recently, anthropologists have argued that the distinction between Montagnais and Naskapi Indians is misleading. It suggests that they are two distinct societies, although in fact they share the same culture. The Indians argue that the terms *Montagnais* and *Naskapi* were wrongly imposed upon them by Europeans, just as the term *Eskimo* was imposed on the Inuit people of northern Canada. Indeed, the Innu themselves stress that they are one people with an extensive network of shared social relations among their communities. For example, all speak Innu-aimun, one of several related dialects of the Cree language. This language is classified by scholars as part of the Algonquian linguistic family. The Innu's culture is similar to other Algonquian-speaking peoples, who inhabit subarctic forest lands from the east coast of Labrador to the Rocky Mountains.

The history of the Indians who inhabit the Quebec-Labrador Peninsula began about 12,000 years ago, when immense ice sheets, known as glaciers, covered much of North America. These glaciers drew water from the oceans, a process that lowered the sea level and exposed stretches of land, including one between Asia and North America. Using this natural bridge, the distant ancestors of the Innu migrated from Siberia across the Bering Strait to what is now Alaska. When the glaciers later began to melt, the descendants of these Indians, who belonged to what scholars call Paleo-Indian culture (paleo is from the Greek word *palaios*, meaning "old"), traveled southward in pursuit of food resources. In this manner, Indians eventually colonized almost all of North and South America.

Archaeologists (scientists who study the remains of past societies) have called the first known Indian society in North America the Clovis culture, named for the Blackwater Draw excavation site near Clovis, New Mexico. (Scholars use such labels to help them organize their research chronologically; the terms are not the actual names of these early people. Indeed, "Clovis" is most often used simply to describe the special type of spear points and arrowheads first unearthed at Blackwater Draw.) Archaeological evidence of the same type from the Canadian province of Nova Scotia indicates that the Indians of the Clovis period reached the northeastern part of North America between 11,000 and 10,000 years ago. These Indians obtained food primarily by hunting caribou, but during the spring and summer they traveled to the coast of the Gulf of St. Lawrence in order to fish and hunt sea mammals and birds. They most likely gathered some of the plant foods available in the region, but archaeological evidence for such activities did not survive.

Soon after these early Indian pioneers had discovered this source of food, they crossed to the Quebec North Shore (the northern bank of the St. Lawrence River), where the coastal resources were equally rich. Archaeologists are not certain when the first people arrived in this part of Quebec. But they speculate that the Indians either crossed the St. Lawrence in some type of boat or traveled up the shore of the river until they reached a point where it was still covered with ice and crossed it on foot.

After these first Indians arrived on the Quebec North Shore, the climate, wildlife, and vegetation of the area began to change. As the glaciers receded toward the northern part of the Quebec-Labrador peninsula, a corridor opened along the coast through which vegetation, wildlife, and finally people migrated from the south. Large populations of sea mammals were present along the coastline, and caribou moved into the region a few centuries after deglaciation.

Beginning in about 5,500 B.C., a cultural change began to take place in the Quebec-Labrador area. Archaeologists have found tools, weapons, and musical instruments dating from this period in the coastal regions of Quebec-Labrador that are of a type, both in style and function, that differed from those made by the previous Indian people. Scholars say that this archaeological evidence is from a period they have labeled as Maritime Archaic. The remains suggest that the new social system probably resulted either from the culmination of slow changes in the previous Indian culture or from the arrival of another cultural group. Archaeologists believe that the people of the Maritime Archaic culture depended heavily on fishing and on hunting seals and migratory waterfowl. But scholars also note the prominence of caribou remains at Maritime Archaic sites. Therefore, it is likely that throughout the year the Indians

A group of Maritime Archaic projectile points. The Indians of this period acquired most of their food from coastal waters in their territory, so these tools were probably used to capture fish and other aquatic animals.

killed caribou along the coast as well as at interior locations where the animals could be intercepted on their migration routes across rivers and lakes.

The Maritime Archaic occupation of Quebec-Labrador was very extensive. The ancient campsites of these people have been found in the interior of the peninsula as well as on the north coast of Labrador. However, the Maritime Archaic people appear to have abandoned the northern coastal areas of Quebec-Labrador about 3,500 years ago. Scholars believe this may have occurred because of cooling climatic conditions and diminished wildlife resources. Scholars also believe that Paleo-Eskimo people moving into the region from the north may have driven the Maritime Archaic Indians inland.

What happened to these peoples after they left the coast is still open to question. Archaeologists believe they may have retreated southward to join other Indian groups on the North Shore of Quebec. Some Maritime Archaic groups may have disappeared entirely or simply got so small that their members joined other existing groups or joined together to form new groups; others may have moved inland to hunt wildlife, such as caribou.

One archaeologist, William Fitzhugh, believes the Maritime Archaic way of life may have survived in the Lake Melville region of Labrador until 3,600 years ago. After this date, however, archaeological evidence suggests that new cultural practices came into being. Fitzhugh calls them Intermediate Period cultures. Archaeologists do not know if these societies consisted of the descendants of the Maritime Archaic Indians or of new arrivals from the northwestern part of Canada. One thing is clear, though. These Indian peoples exploited inland wildlife resources for food far more than the Indians of the Maritime Archaic period or the later Innu.

The one exception was the final Intermediate Period culture to appear in Quebec-Labrador—the Point Revenge culture, which dates from 1,200 to 300 years ago. Archaeologists think that the Point Revenge people may have been the immediate ancestors of the northern Innu groups.

The Point Revenge culture was in many ways similar to that of the Maritime Archaic Indians as well as the contemporary Innu people who live along the Gulf of St. Lawrence. All three groups probably spent the winter inland seeking caribou but moved to the coast each spring to hunt seals and other marine animals.

The Point Revenge Indians used caribou hides to make clothing. According to historical records, women manufactured coats, hoods, pants, moccasins, and leggings from hides with the fur turned inside. The hides were probably cleaned and preserved with the same methods that contemporary Innu employ.

These Indians also used caribou hides to cover their tents. These structures resembled the conical buffalo hide tipis made by Plains Indians in central

Canada and the United States. The Point Revenge Indians may also have covered their tents with birchbark. This is most probably true of the groups that lived in the southern portion of the Quebec-Labrador peninsula, where birch trees are found in great abundance. At Point Revenge sites in the Lake Melville area of central Labrador, the remains of two to three tents have been found. These date from approximately 1,000 to 300 years ago. The bases of these ancient dwellings were oval in shape, and the structures seem to have been covered with skin or bark that was held down with small boulders. In the center of each tent was a ring of cobblestones or slab rocks where the Indians built fires.

By 1,000 years ago, Point Revenge hunting groups occupied most of the Labrador coast south of Saglek Bay and probably most of the interior of the Quebec-Labrador peninsula as well. They remained there until about 500 years ago, when the Thule Inuit people

A 1968 photograph of the excavation of a Point Revenge site on Labrador's north coast. The long, dark objects lying in the pit are the remains of fallen tipi poles.

arrived. Archaeologists think that the Inuit stopped the Point Revenge Indians from hunting and traveling along most of the coast during the summer. Their economic loss was probably great. As a result, the Indians were forced either to confine their hunting to deeper bays and river mouths or to hunt caribou in the interior of the peninsula.

Along the Quebec North Shore, where the Thule Inuit did not penetrate, the Indians apparently continued to rely on marine animals for their food. Scholars assume this is so because the Point Revenge Indians' descendants—the Innu—practiced this method of hunting. Records kept by early European explorers show that Innu groups actively engaged in seal hunting and fishing in the area between the present-day communities of Mingan and Tadoussac.

About 400 years ago, a new source of information about the Quebec-Labrador Innu appeared. It came from European missionaries, fishermen, sailors, and explorers. These travelers

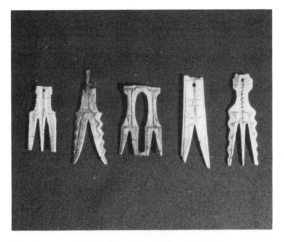

Pendants made from split and polished bone. These adornments were made by members of the Beothuck tribe of Newfoundland. The Beothuck, closely related to the Innu, ceased to exist by the beginning of the 19th century.

wrote about the inhabitants of North America in their journals and created legends and tales about them that soon spread through Europe. But the Innu way of life described by Europeans was changed forever within a few years after their arrival. ▲

A View of Quebec City, *engraved in the early 18th century by the French artist Jean-Baptiste Franquelin. The spired buildings in the center belonged to the various missionary orders, such as the Recollects and the Jesuits, that settled in Quebec. The depiction of the Indians in the foreground has more to do with European fiction about native North Americans than with historical fact.*

A PEOPLE
IN
TRANSITION

Many non-Indians in North America consider the continent's history to have begun with the arrival of their European ancestors. However, the first European explorers to travel across the Atlantic did not find an uninhabited wilderness. On the contrary, they encountered hundreds of Indian groups who had technological, political, and economic systems and religious beliefs significantly different from those of European peoples. But soon after their arrival, these Europeans managed to turn their new home into a "virgin landscape," open to their settlement and exploitation. They did so by causing the death of thousands of Indians through enslavement, warfare, the transmission of deadly European diseases, and the disruption of the Indians' traditional means of obtaining food. The ancestors of the Innu were among the first North American Indians to come under the devastating influence of Europeans.

The first Europeans to arrive in the Quebec-Labrador peninsula were the Vikings (also called Norsemen) from what are today the Scandinavian countries of Norway, Sweden, and Denmark. Between the 8th and the 13th centuries, the Vikings attacked and pillaged many of the towns and cities along the coasts of northern Europe. Their voyages of exploration and conquest led them as far as the shores of Iceland, Greenland, and eventually the mainland of North America.

In about A.D. 1003, Thorvald Eriksson (son of Erik the Red and brother of Leif) and a group of Viking sailors set out, under orders from their leader Leif, from a Norse colony in Greenland and traveled westward. Their aim was to reach the coast of Newfoundland, which Leif had landed on some three years earlier. However, Thorvald and his crew traveled instead to the coast of what is now Labrador. The men sailed

The reconstructed Viking settlement L'Anse aux Meadows, located on the northeast tip of Newfoundland. The camp was established in about A.D. 1000 by Viking explorer Leif Eriksson and his crew. It was Eriksson's brother Thorvald, however, who first encountered the Innu in Labrador.

into Lake Melville, dropped anchor, and went ashore. There they discovered three canoes under which were hiding nine Indian people, referred to in Viking epics as *skraelings*. The Vikings killed all but one of the skraelings, who managed to escape. He presumably ran to his camp and told the people what happened, because later that day a large group of Indians attacked the Vikings in retaliation. During the skirmish, several of the Vikings were killed, including Eriksson. The surviving Norsemen returned to Greenland the following spring to escape the threat of further Indian attacks.

It was not until 500 years later that the next contact between Europeans and the Labrador Indians occurred. In the 1500s, French fishermen encountered Innu at the Strait of Belle Isle, which lies between the mainland and island portions of Newfoundland. Unlike the previous encounter between Indians and Vikings, the Innu's meetings with these Frenchmen were friendly. The fishermen wanted to trade with the Indians rather than fight with them. The Innu were equally interested in the items that the French sailors brought with them. The Frenchmen reported that the Innu believed that the metal goods they obtained from the fishermen possessed supernatural powers. They also thought that the Europeans' huge ships were floating islands.

In 1534, another Frenchman, explorer Jacques Cartier, traveled up the St. Lawrence River and disembarked on the Gaspé Peninsula. Upon his landing, Cartier claimed the area in the name of France. He then traveled to southern Labrador, where he met with several Innu people near the present-day town of Natashquan.

During the early 1540s, contact between Europeans and the Innu increased drastically. People from the Basque region of north-central Spain and south-central France established a whale and cod fishery in the Gran Baya (Grand Bay), the name they gave to the Strait of Belle Isle. Between 1545 and 1585, more than 1,000 Basque whalers and longshoremen worked in the region, sometimes living there for up to half the year. Historian Lope de Isasti noted that Innu would "talk and associate with our men and help to prepare the fish on shore in exchange for a little bread, biscuit and cider that they do not have over there." The Indians would

An engraving that depicts the various stages of fish processing practiced by European commercial fishermen in eastern Canada.

also trade furs to the Basques in exchange for iron tools and utensils. Relations between the two groups were generally friendly. For example, the Innu often warned the Basques of impending attacks by Inuit with whom the Basques were not on good terms.

After 1560, Basque whalers and French fishermen, whose numbers in the region had also increased, began to move farther west into the Gulf of St. Lawrence. They may have engaged in whaling and in trading for furs with the Indians in the area of present-day Tadoussac. The traders were particularly

interested in acquiring beaver furs, which could be sold for high prices in European markets.

The Innu had a clear advantage over the Europeans in the early years of the fur trade. A large number of French traders had to compete for the Indians' supply of furs. Therefore, the Innu were able to play the traders off against one another and drive up the amount of goods that the Europeans would trade for the pelts.

By the end of the 16th century, Tadoussac was the most important fur-trading center in North America, and

French explorer Samuel de Champlain's 1613 map of the fort at Tadoussac. The houses (letter D) on the small island mark the spot where Innu hunters camped when they came to trade with the French.

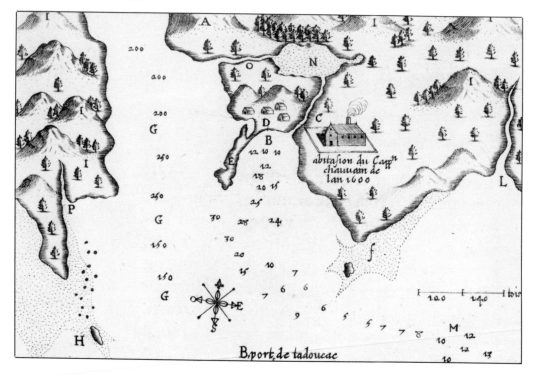

the Innu had almost exclusive control of trade there. Tadoussac's location contributed to its prominence. Situated in what is now the Province of Quebec, just north of the mouth of the Saguenay River, it was near the junction of many of the traditional routes used by the Indians of the region. Coastal Indian traders had often used the area's waterways during their expeditions to trade with Indian groups living in the interior of the Quebec-Labrador peninsula. Archaeological evidence suggests that by the late 16th century furs were reaching Tadoussac from such distant inland locations as present-day southern Ontario and the region around James Bay.

In 1604, the French decided to take full advantage of the fortunes to be made in the fur trade. Under the direction of King Henry IV, New France—the portion of North America claimed by France—was officially declared a French colony. In that same year, French explorer Pierre du Gua established the new colony's first settlement—Île de Ste. Croix in New Brunswick.

Four years later, explorers Samuel de Champlain and François du Pont Gravé arrived in Tadoussac and asked the Innu there for permission to establish a settlement farther up the St. Lawrence River. The place the Frenchmen chose was called the Narrows of Quebec, the site of present-day Quebec City. Champlain and Pont Gravé wanted to develop extensive trading relations with the Huron and the Algonquian Indians living to the west of the

A 17th-century engraving of a French fur trader. The man is wearing snowshoes, a means of travel adopted by Europeans from the Indians.

narrows because they sought more furs than the Innu could provide. The Frenchmen also hoped to break the Innu's monopoly on the fur trade in the region, which naturally was more favorable to the Indians.

The Innu supported the Frenchmen's proposal and agreed to allow the French to construct the settlement. The

Innu hoped that a French presence nearby would provide a protective shield between them and the five tribes of Iroquois Indians, who lived just south of the St. Lawrence River. The Iroquois had been staging raids on Innu settlements because they wanted to gain control of the region's fur trade.

Sometime after 1570, increasing attacks by one Iroquois tribe—the Mohawk—had led the Innu and several other Algonquian-speaking tribes to form a military alliance. The French formally allied themselves with these Indian groups because they wanted to ensure a regular supply of furs from them. The French also had to continue to allow the Innu to act as middlemen between the traders and the Indians living to the west.

The Innu carefully guarded their position in the fur trade. In 1608, Champlain complained in his journal about their tight control of transactions be-

Champlain's engraving of a 1609 battle, depicting the defeat of an Iroquois war party by his soldiers and their Innu and Algonquin allies. The Iroquois warriors are located inside the fort.

tween the western Indian groups and the French traders:

> This is the region to which our savages go with the merchandise we give them in exchange for their furs, such as beaver, marten, lynx, and otter which are found there in large numbers and which they bring to our ships. These northern tribes tell our Indians that they see the salt sea. . . . I have often desired to explore it, but have been unable to do so without the natives, who have been unwilling that I or any of our people should go with them.

France's alliance with the Algonquian speakers sometimes required the French to aid the Indians in warfare with their enemies. In 1609 and 1610, for example, Champlain and his men fought alongside the Innu and their Indian allies during their battles with the Mohawk. These combined forces successfully defeated the Mohawk raiding parties that had been patrolling the St. Lawrence. The Frenchmen's guns particularly terrified the Mohawk, who had never before seen or heard European weapons.

The Innu came to pay an increasingly heavy price for their alliance with the French, however. The French were not content simply to coexist with their Indian allies. Instead, they planned to conquer the Innu and take their lands. One intention of this policy was to make the Innu abandon trade in their traditional hunting economy for a "more civilized" agricultural (and Eu-

ropean) way of life. In this way, the French could restrict the Indians to small plots of land and take control of their huge hunting territories. The condescending attitude of the French toward the Innu culture and their desire to destroy it would become a recurring theme in the subsequent history of the Innu.

Champlain was one of the first Europeans to attempt to change the Innu. After 1620, when he began to actively promote the settlement of New France, he tried to persuade the Innu to learn French, to become farmers, and to convert to Christianity. He even went so far as to attempt to appoint the Innu's chiefs. Champlain argued that it was necessary for French colonists to live alongside Innu in order to encourage them to give up their "filthy habits, loose morals, and uncivilized ways." As an official of the French crown, Champlain also thought he had a right to tell the Indians how to run their affairs. Because Champlain believed that the Innu's culture was so worthless, he assumed that the Indians would quickly choose to abandon their traditions when presented with the "civilized" ways of the French.

The Innu, however, felt quite differently about the matter. They continually rejected Champlain's attempts to change their way of life. The Innu eventually became so angered at Champlain's meddling, as well as at the high prices charged by his French trading company, that they helped a group of Englishmen led by David Kirk attack the French settlement at Quebec City. The French were defeated and surrendered the settlement to the English in July 1629. France did not regain control of Quebec City until three years later.

Champlain was not the only Frenchman who tried to modify the culture of the Innu. French missionaries did so as well. The first clerics to live among the Indians were Catholic priests of the Recollect order, who in 1615 established a mission at Quebec City. In 1625, a second mission was founded by a group of Jesuit priests. At first the Innu may have viewed these missionaries as shamans and may have viewed the ceremonies performed by the priests, such as baptism, in terms of the Indians' own religious practices. In these early years, they certainly did not regard baptism and other Catholic rituals as a threat to their traditions.

Both the Recollects and the Jesuits advocated "civilizing" the Innu. But the two religious orders differed in their view of how this was to be achieved. The Recollects believed the Innu would have to live among the Europeans in order to be effectively converted. In contrast, the Jesuits stressed that the Innu had to be isolated from European settlers whenever possible. These priests believed that the settlers would exert a negative influence upon the Indians by encouraging them to adopt a variety of European vices.

The Jesuits, however, recognized that it was important for the French to maintain their trade relationship with the Indians. Prior to 1663, the French government provided no money for the support of its colonies in North America. Therefore, the fur trade, which could only continue with the aid of the Indians, was the sole source of financial support for New France. The fur trade also gave individual colonists an opportunity to acquire great wealth and high social status. In the long run, the Jesuits may have planned to compel Innu to live in settled communities and to abandon hunting, but in the short term the priests had to cooperate with the goals of the fur-trading companies.

As a result of the fur trade, the Innu people living to the west of Tadoussac made important changes in their economy. By 1623, Innu groups at Tadoussac and Quebec no longer manufactured their traditional birchbark baskets and stone adzes. Instead, they increasingly began to use copper kettles and iron axes, which they acquired from French traders in exchange for their furs. The Indians also began to wear European-style garments over their traditional skin clothes because the French clothing was more comfortable in wet weather. These Innu continued to make traditional birchbark canoes, but they also bought French-made longboats (30-foot-long wooden crafts with a single mast) for coastal travel.

Other, more serious changes were also beginning to occur among the western Innu. By the 1630s, a major threat to the Indians' position as middlemen in the fur trade had begun to take hold. The Innu's neighbors to the

A View of the Jesuits' College and Church, *painted in 1759 by the English artist Charles Grignon. The Jesuits were among the religious missionary orders that encouraged the Innu to adopt European values.*

west—the Huron—had sidestepped them and had established a relationship as rival middlemen between the French and the Indian groups in the Ottawa River valley. In addition, Innu trappers had by this time seriously depleted the beaver population in the area between Quebec City and Tadoussac. The population of other game animals, in particular moose and elks, had declined drastically as well.

These shortages further contributed to the deteriorating economy of the Innu. Unable to acquire meat from their traditional sources, the Indians became increasingly dependent on foodstuffs supplied by the French, including maize, dried peas, crackers, prunes, and flour. More and more western Innu were forced to seek help from the French missionaries and traders.

Europeans—outbreaks of epidemic diseases. These afflictions—including smallpox, measles, influenza, chicken pox, mumps, typhoid, scarlet fever, diphtheria, and syphilis—had been unknown in North America before the arrival of Europeans. As a result, North American Indians had no natural immunity to the diseases and died by the thousands. In 1632, the year the French regained control of Quebec from the British, the Innu were struck by an epidemic that may have been smallpox, measles, or influenza. This outbreak was followed in 1639 by a smallpox

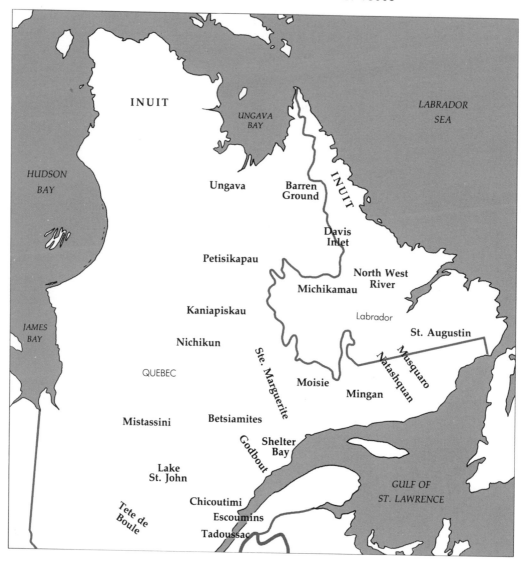

INUIT

UNGAVA
BAY

LABRADOR
SEA

HUDSON
BAY

Ungava

Barren
Ground

INUIT

Davis
Inlet

Petisikapau

North West
River

Michikamau

Kaniapiskau

Labrador

JAMES
BAY

Nichikun

St. Augustin

QUEBEC

Ste. Marguerite

Moisie

Musquaro

Natashquan

Mingan

Mistassini

Betsiamites

Godbout

Shelter
Bay

Lake
St. John

GULF OF
ST. LAWRENCE

Tete de
Boule

Chicoutimi

Escoumins

Tadoussac

epidemic that raged throughout the St. Lawrence River valley, killing hundreds of Indians in the region. By the end of the 1630s, the Innu groups of the Quebec City region began to believe that the French planned nothing short of their extermination so that they could gain control of the Indians' land.

The declining population of the western Innu made them extremely vulnerable to their enemies. At this time, the Mohawk renewed their raids against Innu settlements, particularly their hunting encampments, along the St. Lawrence River. In 1629, the Mohawk destroyed the Algonkian and Montagnais village at Trois-Rivières. Raids such as this were much more devastating than those that had occurred in the past because in 1639 the Iroquois had begun to acquire guns from Dutch traders. The Mohawk were often joined in their attacks by two other Iroquois tribes—the Oneida and the Onondaga. The raiding Iroquois groups wanted both to seize the Innu's furs and to obtain access to their hunting grounds. These tribes needed new territory in which to hunt and trap because they had depleted the wildlife in their own territories.

The drastic population losses and increased Iroquois raids soon forced the Tadoussac Innu to give up their exclusive position as trading envoys to the French. Although the Innu had previously tried to prevent other Indians from trading directly with the French, they now invited other tribes to join in the exchange network. The new groups that came to trade at Tadoussac included the Papinachois and Betsiamites Innu, who lived farther east along the Quebec North Shore.

In the 1650s, the Iroquois raids intensified and spread farther into eastern Innu territory. In 1652, a group of Innu and a Jesuit priest named Jacques Buteux at an Innu camp near Sillery, were attacked by an Iroquois raiding party. The survivors fled to Tadoussac. Five years later, the Iroquois attacked several Innu groups farther up the Saguenay River. During the raids, the Ouakwiechiwek, Outabitibek, and Kepatawanejach bands of Innu were broken up into smaller units that were forced to take refuge in more distant areas. The Innu occasionally attempted to combat their enemies by joining their forces with those of the Micmac and other allied neighbors, but such efforts generally had few lasting effects.

The attacks on the Tadoussac Innu reached a climax in 1661 when their settlement at Tadoussac was burned and destroyed by the Iroquois. The Iroquois then turned their attention to the Innu of the Lake St. John area. There they attacked and killed or drove away the Porcupine band of Innu. In 1662, the same plight befell the Cree living between Tadoussac and Hudson Bay. This group had never before encountered the Iroquois and were therefore completely unprepared for the attack.

As the Iroquois attacks increased, so did the number of Indians seeking refuge in Quebec City. In 1663 alone, more than 300 Algonquian speakers, including Micmac and Innu Indians, sought aid and safety there. Many of these Innu refugees had never before met with the French, but they preferred life with these strangers to certain death at the hands of the deadly Iroquois.

Events in the late 1660s brought the final blow to the Innu's livelihood. At this time, a young French trader named Médard Chouart des Groseilliers was arrested and fined by the colonial government for trading in furs without a license. In retaliation, he arranged a meeting with the English, told them of the wealth of furs to be had to the north in the Hudson Bay region, and promised to lead a British expedition there. The voyage was such a success that England's king Charles II granted to the expedition's financial backers exclusive rights to all the furs in a 1.5-million-square-mile area. The backers called their new venture the Hudson's Bay Company. This new company quickly became a major threat to the French fur trade in the region east and south of Hudson Bay.

The Innu's political and economic power, afforded to them by their position in the fur trade, vanished almost immediately. For example, the Indian groups near Lake Mistassini had in the past acquired European goods from the Tadoussac Innu. Now, however, they were able to trade directly with the British, who offered them better prices. As a result, trade between the Innu and the French soon began to suffer.

The first page of the charter presented in 1670 by France's king Charles II to the founders of the Hudson's Bay Company.

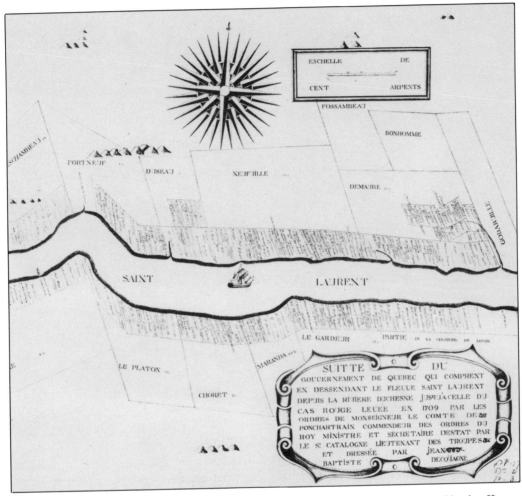

An early-18th-century map of seigneuries, *or land grants, in New France. Charles II presented these tracts to French merchants, bureaucrats, and military men in return for their service to France.*

Although the volume of exchange was diminished, the French continued to trade with the Innu groups located along the Quebec North Shore during the final decades of the 17th century. In 1663, the French created a system of land grants known as *seigneury*, through which they established many trading operations. French merchants, bureaucrats, and military men, called *seigneurs*, were awarded tracts of land in North America by the French crown as payment for services they had performed for France. Churches could also

An engraving of the 1759 battle for Quebec City between British and French forces. France's defeat in this episode of the French and Indian War helped ensure Britain's complete takeover of New France in 1763.

apply and receive grants. Seigneurs were given these properties for life and could pass them on to their heirs. Seigneurs also received exclusive rights to collect certain resources on specific portions of the Quebec North Shore and to trade with the Innu. Many trading posts, called *postes du roi* (king's posts), sprang up in the Indians' territory as a result of the seigneurial system.

Sept-Îles, one of the earliest seigneuries, became an important center of trade in 1674. It was strategically located at the mouth of the Moisie River, an important travel route to the interior. Many Innu congregated there each summer to trade their beaver skins for European goods. Shortly thereafter, in

1679, Jacques de Lalande and Louis Jolliet became seigneurs of Mingan, a territory about 100 miles east of Sept-Îles. In addition to fishing for cod, sealing, and whaling, the French living at Mingan conducted an energetic fur trade with the Innu.

Few details are available about the relations between the Innu and the French during the 1700s. Scholars do know that these groups continued to trade using their own goods, rather than currency, to acquire other goods. The Indians brought furs to the postes du roi along the coast, where they exchanged them for food, pots and kettles, textiles, tools, and other European-made products. Some of these items, such as muskets and traps, were used by the Indians for hunting. Trade between the French and the Indians at the postes du roi remained lucrative for several years, but this success was not to last.

Tensions between the French and English steadily escalated throughout the early 18th century, erupting into a conflict known as the Seven Years' War. The armies of these rivals battled in both Europe and North America, where the conflict is referred to as the French and Indian War (1754–63). At its conclusion, the French were defeated by their British rivals, despite the military aid provided by France's Indian allies. Under the terms of surrender, agreed upon in the 1763 Treaty of Paris, New France came under British rule.

The British crown renamed its new colony Quebec and imposed British rule on the French settlers that lived there. In 1791, the British crown attempted to silence the increasing protests by splitting Quebec into two colonies—Upper Canada and Lower Canada. Upper Canada, the area north of the Great Lakes, was populated mostly by Indians and British settlers and was to be governed under British law. Lower Canada, the area surrounding the upper St. Lawrence River and the traditional homeland of the Innu, had a majority of French colonists. Therefore, although it had a British parliamentary system, the province followed French civil law. Each colony was presided over by a lieutenant governor and a legislative council, the members of which were appointed by the British crown, as well as an elected legislative assembly. The two colonies were later combined under the 1840 Act of Union and renamed the Province of Canada.

Initially, these political changes had little effect on the Innu. Most of their contact with non-Indians continued to center around trade. But, in 1842, the Innu began to feel the impact of the Canadian government. In that year, the legislature of Lower Canada voted to open the Saguenay River region to settlement. This opened the door to steady immigration by Quebecois (French Canadians) into the western parts of Innu territory. In 1844, there were fewer than 1,500 Quebecois in the area; by 1851, there were more than 5,000. Many of the first settlers moved to Innu territory to work in newly opened lumber camps and sawmills. Others began to establish farms.

Quebecois settlement and industrial development in the Saguenay area took important hunting territory away from the Innu and contributed to the disappearance of their wildlife resources. Similar problems were soon encountered by Innu in other areas, especially those on the Quebec North Shore, as lumbering activities moved into various coastal lands. This rapid influx of Quebecois to Innu territory would prove devastating to the Indians throughout the last half of the 19th century. ▲

Two Innu women pose in front of a canoe, photographed in the early 20th century.

3

A THREATENED
WAY OF LIFE

The invasion of the Innu's territory by European immigrants motivated many Indians to take action. In the mid-19th century, they sent several petitions pleading their case to the colonial government. The Innu hoped that the documents would prompt the government to help them retain control of their remaining lands and to offer them compensation for those lands already lost.

One petition, written in Innu-ai-mun, was signed by 106 Innu from the upper Saguenay area in 1848. Three Innu chiefs, Tumas Mesituapamuskan, Jusep Kakanukus, and Pasil Tnishien-apen, presented it in person to the governor-general of Canada. They then described to the official the extent of the Innu's loss of land and the resulting state of distress among their people. The chiefs further explained that whites and other Indians had depleted food and fuel resources and started forest fires in their territory. As a result, the Innu's lands had become so poor that

they now had to purchase large quantities of food and clothing—things they had once provided for themselves. The chiefs informed the governor that they were shocked that their land had been taken from them. The Innu saw themselves as the rightful masters of the territory as decreed by God.

In accordance with the main purpose of their visit, the chiefs presented the governor-general with a number of demands. They required that the colonial government pass legislation that would allow the Innu to use the land bordering the Peribonca River and the entrance to the great discharge from Lake St. John for their annual spring gatherings; give them the royalties collected by the government from traders, forestry operations, and the sale of the land; make them the masters of the trading posts at Tadoussac, Chicoutimi, and Lake St. John when the leases expired on them; prevent other Indians from hunting in their territory; give them agricultural equipment; and give them presents such as those provided by the government to other Indian groups. The Innu leaders had carefully thought out these demands, which, if met, would allow the Indians to become self-sufficient once again.

In 1849, the assistant commissioner of Crown lands reported on the Indians' petition and recommended that they be given land and funds. However, the government took no action until 1851, when it passed the Victoria Act 14 and 15. The act stated the government's intent to reserve 230,000 acres of land for the Indians in the lower portion of Canada. In 1853, a second document reserved a tract of 16,000 acres along the Peribonca River specifically for the Indians who hunted in the Saguenay River basin and its tributaries. An additional 4,000 acres along Lake St. John at the mouth of the Metapetshuan River was also reserved for Indian use.

Three more years passed before the government was officially able to establish its first reserve for the Innu, however. The process was delayed because the Innu decided to exchange the land designated for them in 1853, probably because of an influx of Quebecois settlers there. They chose a new tract bordering the Ouiatchouanish River at a

A mid-19th-century watercolor of a French Canadian family's homestead in the province of Quebec.

site called Pointe Bleue. The government agreed to reserve Pointe Bleue for the Indians in 1856. Pointe Bleue soon replaced a post on the Metapetshuan River as the center of Innu trade.

Throughout the 1850s, the colonial government developed legislation to compel its Indian population to adopt non-Indian ways and assimilate into mainstream Canadian culture. With this goal in mind, it passed in 1857 the Act for the Gradual Civilization of the Indian Tribes in the Canadas, which encouraged Indians to give up their traditions. Other acts passed at this time reflected another preoccupation of policymakers of the period—the creation of legal mechanisms by which Indian land could be opened up for non-Indian settlement.

The eastward push of Quebecois settlers and industrialists affected other Innu besides those in the Saguenay area. Their neighbors on the Quebec North Shore east of Tadoussac also felt pressured as forestry operations penetrated their territory in the mid-19th century. In response, the North Shore Innu sent a petition to the government in 1845 asking for reserve land in the region between Betsiamites and Outardes bays. They did not receive an answer, so they sent a delegation to Montreal the following year; but still their demands went unacknowledged.

In 1848, the fortunes of the Innu took a turn for the better. Several priests of the Oblate order living at a mission at Les Escoumins offered to act as intermediaries between the Innu and the government. The clergymen did so because their Indian neighbors in the Saguenay and Pointe-des-Monts region were in particularly great distress that year. The Indians' annual seal hunt had been very unsuccessful, so they were in dire need of food and other supplies. The Oblates persuaded the government to provide money for flour, clothing, and ammunition for the Indians at Chicoutimi, a post located about 50 miles up the Saguenay River. Innu from all along the coast traveled inland to obtain their share of the government supplies.

The following year, the Oblates again demanded assistance from the government on behalf of the Innu. However, their demands soon began to reflect the missionaries' self-interest and their own ideas about what was best for the Indians. The Oblates shared the philosophy proposed 200 years before by Champlain and the Jesuits— that the Innu must be "civilized." The Oblates believed that the Indians could be saved only if they gave up their nomadic hunting existence and in its place adopted an agricultural (and European-style) way of life.

One example of the Oblates' abuse of their position as middlemen can be seen in an 1850 petition sent by the bishop of Quebec to the government. In it, the clergyman argued that the Innu no longer had an adequate means of making a living by hunting and fishing because their wildlife resources had been depleted by Quebecois settlers and by forestry operations. He stated that some of the revenue the govern-

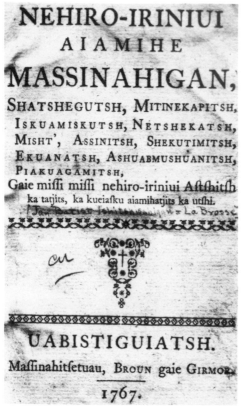

NEHIRO-IRINIUI
AIAMIHE
MASSINAHIGAN,

SHATSHEGUTSH, MITINEKAPITSH,
ISKUAMISKUTSH, NETSHEKATSH,
MISHT', ASSINITSH, SHEKUTIMITSH,
EKUANATSH, ASHUABMUSHUANITSH,
PIAKUAGAMITSH,
Gaie miſſi miſſi nehiro-iriniui Aſtſhitſh
ka tatjits, ka kueiaſku aiamihatjits ka utſhi.

UABISTIGUIATSH.

Maſſinahitſetuau, BROUN gaie GIRMOR.

1767.

The first page of a Christian prayer book in the Innu language. In English, the title reads, Book of Prayers for the Men of the Nations.

ment earned from the exploitation of Indian land ought to be used to provide the Innu with agricultural equipment. The bishop also pointed out that the Indians would not become successful farmers unless the Oblates were able to live with and supervise them. Such supervision, he argued, would allow the Oblates to "force them to profit from the benefits provided by the government."

The government agreed to many of the missionaries' demands. In 1861, it established a 63,000-acre reserve for the Innu on the Betsiamites River. During the fall of 1862, the Oblates permanently moved their mission from Les Escoumins to Betsiamites. The mission attracted the remaining Innu at Tadoussac and many others from nearby settlements. By the mid-1860s, 125 to 200 families were based at Betsiamites. The Oblates called their mission there the "capital of the savage people."

Unfortunately, the Innu that moved to the mission did not find their lives significantly improved. In fact, evidence suggests that their condition worsened. The concentration of people at the Betsiamites mission and trading post promoted the spread of disease. Between 1863 and 1911, 10 epidemics struck Betsiamites, occurring most often during the summer, when most of the Indians were on the reserve. According to historian Helene Bedard, a terrible outbreak of smallpox in 1868 coincided with the failure of the Hudson's Bay Company to provide advances (provisions on credit) to Innu hunters. When the epidemic hit at the beginning of August, it killed 25 people. But 2 weeks later it took 52 more people, almost 10 percent of the entire population of the reserve. Many left for the country to hunt without provisions but were forced to return to the reserve in the winter because they were starving.

The Betsiamites Innu's seafood resources also began to fail them by the beginning of the 1860s. During the late

1840s and 1850s, the Canadian government had introduced legislation that regulated the Indians' harvest of wildlife and provided for the sale of fishing rights to non-Indians in the rivers along the Quebec North Shore. The leases prohibited the Innu from fishing in those areas and thereby deprived the Indians of an important food source. The Innu actively opposed the government's fishing regulations and in 1858 claimed ownership of the Godbout, Betsiamites, Moisie, and Mingan rivers. But their protests appear to have had virtually no effect whatsoever. Authorities seized the catches of and arrested many Indians who tried to defend their fishing rights.

The number of Canadian salmon-fishing posts grew rapidly along the coast. As a result, the salmon stocks of many North Shore rivers had drastically declined by 1864. In 1868, Charles Arnaud, a priest at the Oblate mission at Betsiamites, wrote that "the government is killing these poor Indians and reducing them to misery with its fishing regulations." The priest also noted that the winter had been especially difficult because "provisions were lacking, and they suffered crudely from hunger. One or two died of hunger in the forest, while most of the others returned poor, thin, sick."

The government's disruption of the lives of the Innu increased after 1867. In this year, the British government passed the British North America Act,

An engraving of Indian hunters shooting seals on the Moise River. During the 19th century, non-Indians took over many of the Innu's traditional hunting and fishing territories.

which united the Province of Canada and the British colonies of Nova Scotia and New Brunswick to create the Dominion of Canada. (The Province of Canada became the modern-day provinces of Quebec and Ontario.) One clause in the act gave the new federal government of Canada exclusive responsibilty for "Indians and Lands Reserved for Indians." This clause laid the legal groundwork for a series of "Indian Acts," which still define the country's

Oblate father Charles Arnaud was a priest at the Betsiamites Mission, where many Innu sought refuge and provisions when non-Indians overran their hunting grounds.

policies toward its native peoples. The acts determined the nature of the political institutions that would represent Canadian Indians and, most important, made the Indians wards of the state, thus limiting their legal rights. "Status Indians"—the legal designation of most of the Indians of Canada—were in essence deprived of any meaningful control over their lives. Most of the Innu were regarded as status Indians, with the exception of those groups based in Newfoundland, which would not become part of the Dominion of Canada until 1949.

Throughout the final decades of the 19th century, the Innu at the Betsiamites reserve found their traditional way of life more and more difficult to maintain. Forestry operations continued to move eastward into Innu territory. In 1889, a logging company was even permitted to cut timber on the reserve itself. Logging deforested large areas along the North Shore as well as in the Saguenay River and Lake St. John regions. Forest fires also contributed greatly to the deforestation. In 1895, geologist Albert P. Low estimated that fires had ravaged one-half of the forests of the Quebec-Labrador peninsula. Logging and forest fires together took an enormous toll on the wildlife population and therefore eroded the Innu's hunting economy.

As a conservation measure, the government forbade the Innu living in the Betsiamites region to trap beavers between 1896 and 1900. Beavers, which priests called the Indians' "daily

A late-19th-century lithograph of the Procession of the Indians at the mission at Sept-Îles. Today, a version of this ritual is practiced among the Innu of La Romaine.

bread," had traditionally provided the Innu with a large amount of meat—about 17.4 pounds per animal. Therefore, the regulations heightened the food shortages among the Indians, as did illegal trapping by non-Indian hunters. These people often used strychnine, a poison, to kill beavers, foxes, and other fur-bearing animals. This practice further devastated the wildlife population because strychnine could kill large numbers of animals in a short time.

Food shortages grew to tragic proportions among the Innu. The Indians continued to seek food in their traditional manner, but many were reduced to a state of starvation. The reserve at Betsiamites soon became a home for the sick and elderly. The mission there became one of the most important on the Quebec North Shore, providing its charges with what relief it could.

Farther east, Musquaro was probably the most frequented lower North Shore mission. Musquaro was located just 25 miles west of La Romaine and had been visited by Innu since 1710, when the French established a fortified trading post there. Oblate priests began

A 19th-century etching of Naskapi traders at the Hudson's Bay Company trading post in Mingan. Innu hunters spent increasing amounts of time acquiring furs for trade, and they and their families came to depend on trading posts for many of their everyday needs.

to arrive at the post in about 1850. Thereafter, various groups that hunted and trapped in the drainage basins of the nearby rivers traveled to the Musquaro trading post each spring to trade furs and to attend services at the mission. During their visits, Indian couples married and newborn babies were baptized by the mission priests. They also participated in an annual ritual that is now referred to as the Procession of the Indians.

Today, in La Romaine and other Quebec North Shore villages, the purpose of this ritual is to bless a prospective hunt and all the objects required for it. The ritual integrates Christian traditions with the Innu hunting culture. Symbolic samples of hunting tools and supplies—such as salt, flour, tea, sugar, and candles—and decorated canoes are lined up and sprinkled with holy water. Senior members of the community, the chief, and other representatives of the band council then carry effigies of the Virgin Mary in a procession to an outdoor altar. The procession then marches from the church to an altar located on a hill overlooking the community. Young men intermittently fire guns into the air as the procession moves to and from the altar. An outdoor mass is conducted by the village elders before the rest of the community. The ritual is held late in the summer just before the hunters and their families leave for the country.

At the beginning of the 20th century, virtually all of the Innu on the Quebec coast between Sept-Îles and St. Augustin maintained their hunting and trapping way of life. But like their relatives farther to the west, these Indians found it increasingly difficult to maintain their traditional ways as the years went by. Their economic difficulties had started in the late 19th century as increasing numbers of non-Indians moved into the Indians' territory. By the early 1900s, there were enough new settlers in the region to seriously threaten Innu food resources. The most serious difficulties were created by non-Indian trappers and fishermen.

Canadian lumberers on the St. John River. Non-Indian forestry operations forced many Innu families to relocate to small parcels of land which the Canadian government had reserved for them.

Innu traders, photographed in 1903 outside the Hudson's Bay Company post at Davis Inlet.

As early as 1868, Indian traders at Mingan had begun to receive relief payments from the government. But in the early 1900s, as their income from the fur sales decreased, Indian families in the area became more and more dependent on government rations. A few decades later, this dependency was almost total. According to John Fiset, the Hudson's Bay Company (HBC) manager at La Romaine in 1938, the meager government rations had become by that time essential to the Indians' survival. Most Innu families ran out of money in the summer of each year and thereafter had to live by catching fish, hunting birds, and receiving government rations. The Indians had to purchase provisions for the fall hunting season on credit from the HBC, but the company's credit system began to deteriorate as Innu families were increasingly unable to repay their debts. According to Fiset:

Though the credit advances given to the Indians by the Company were small, they had trouble enough paying them. Most of them had to be continually pressed. Nevertheless, usually by the end of the fiscal year [May 31st], most of the Indians had paid their debts. . . . Credit was more or less at the discretion of the manager, who of course, knew, or was supposed to know, about the capabilities of his Indians as trappers. . . . In the case of a complete failure of his trapping, a good Indian customer was again advanced funds for the same amount, others also were but at a reduced rate. Nobody was ever completely cut off. The amounts advanced were very small—it varied between $25 and $100, maybe $125.

The Innu in central Labrador had similar problems during the early 1900s. Some of the Indians' best trapping grounds had been encroached upon by Settlers (people of mixed European and Inuit ancestry) and by Newfoundlanders during the late 19th century. By 1900, the Innu had begun to complain to the HBC that Settlers were invading their territory. Armed conflict occurred on at least one occasion. This incident, which took place near Churchill Falls, was described by a Settler named Bert Blake:

Myself, William Montague, Henry Groves, Charlie Goudie and Arch Goudie were the first white men that went in there to trap among the Indians . . . they didn't like it. They tried to drive us out every way. . . . We were young men then and we didn't care how much, we stuck it out all winter. . . . Arch Goudie had just struck up his [trap] lines when six Indians came out one evening in the afternoon. They were so cross about us stealing their trapping. They had gone to Seven Islands [Sept-Îles] and come back again after the winter. There were six men and they were so cross that one man took his gun and held it to Arch's head while the others robbed away all his grub and burned down his tilt [a small log cabin]. I came there a little while after, and I didn't know this happened so there we were left without food, only a little bit I had.

In 1909, the Innu explained their problems with the Settlers to the Revillon Frères Trading Company, which was located across the North West River from the HBC at the North West River settlement. The company manager, Raoul Thevenet, reported in that year:

The territory at and around North West River as far as Hopedale toward the coast [about 100 miles to the north] had been the best of the Indian hunting ground for generations past, but these last few years the [Settlers] . . . and Newfoundlanders have been making a regular business of trapping, some of them having as many as three to six hundred traps set during the hunting season. In doing this they have overrun the Indian hunting grounds. The Indians are continually complaining to me about the matter, for, as hunting is their only means of living, they are getting poorer every year. Indeed but for the relief which has been given them at the expense of the Government of Canada some of them would surely have starved. They are becoming very bitter against the white trappers and any year trouble may break out.

The Labrador Innu's difficulties with the Settlers were compounded by other serious problems as the century progressed. Fur prices fell sharply, and at the same time the population of local caribou drastically declined. By the 1940s, the Indians' condition was as desperate as that of their western relatives. Many Indians were reluctant to travel far inland for fear of starvation and of the deadly diseases that struck at this time and took many lives. By their own standards, the Indians were living in extreme poverty. In order to survive, they increasingly had to seek assistance from the government of Newfoundland.

After World War II ended in 1945, the Newfoundland government began to show a more active interest in the inhabitants of Labrador, including the Innu. The government developed several policies to try to alleviate the Indians' poverty and health problems. One policy called for their relocation to an area that was still rich enough in resources for them to live off the land. For example, in 1948, the Indians who frequented the area between Davis Inlet and Indian House Lake were moved to the Inuit community of Nutak on the north coast of Labrador. The transplanted Innu were then pressured by the government to take up commercial fishing. The Indians found this plan as unacceptable as the barren environment surrounding Nutak. They soon returned to the Davis Inlet region.

In 1949, Newfoundland gave up its status as an independent country to become a province in the Canadian confederation. This arrangement posed a problem for the Innu of Labrador. Unlike their relatives in Quebec, the Labrador groups were not made status Indians under the Canadian government's Indian Act of 1876 because they did not live within the country's borders at that time. However, now that Newfoundland was part of Canada, the question arose as to whether the Labrador Innu should be given this legal status as their relatives in the Province of Quebec had been. After some debate, the Canadian and Newfoundland governments chose not to designate the Labrador Innu as status Indians but to make them full-fledged Canadian citizens instead. The governments' decision was probably motivated by a desire to integrate the Indians into mainstream Canadian society. Unfortunately, it also excluded the Labrador Innu from the expanding range of programs and services provided to status Indians by the Canadian government. Citizenship did provide the Labrador Innu with the right to vote, a right that other Canadian Indians did not receive until the 1960s. But voting for local representatives most likely had little relevance to them at this time because they still spent much of the year hunting and trapping in the interior of the Quebec-Labrador peninsula.

By the 1950s, the Labrador Innu were in such a terrible state that the Canadian and Newfoundland governments decided to become more directly involved in the Indians' lives. Both governments recommended relocating the Indians to government-built communities where they would live year-round. Two government officials—Walter G. Rockwood, the provincial director of the Division of Northern Labrador Affairs (DNLA), and Anthony Paddon, the director of the International Grenfell Association Hospital in North West River—greatly influenced the implementation of this and other policies designed to help the Labrador Indians during the 1950s and 1960s. Both men supported industrial development as the solution to the economic and social problems of the region. The Indians' traditional practices of hunting and fishing were seen as incompatible with this vision. Therefore, the policy included plans for the rapid integration,

A late-19th-century Innu hunting camp at Grand Lake in the interior of Labrador. During this time, dwellings were made from wooden poles covered with caribou hides. Today, tents are equipped with ready-made canvas covers.

A view of government-built housing in the Innu settlement at Sept-Îles.

or assimilation, of the Innu into mainstream Canadian society.

In both Quebec and Labrador, provincial government officials believed that education was one of the best vehicles for assimilating Indians. For example, one document written in 1956 for the Newfoundland government stated:

> The Eskimos and Indians cannot continue to exist as isolated minorities but must ultimately be integrated into the general body of our Society. A vigorous programme in Welfare and Education, particularly the latter is required to match the Health programme already underway, and to prepare these minorities for the Society of the Future.

But, as Rockwood noted in 1959, this integration would not be simple because many Indians opposed the idea:

> [It should not] be imagined that the mere teaching of English, or even trades, will solve all the problems, because, as experience elsewhere has shown, there are deeply rooted psychological attitudes to be overcome. There is not an easy, short-

term solution, but only the slow and sometimes painful way of integration and even this is a nasty word to a great many of the Indians themselves.

Nevertheless, the Department of Indian Affairs (DIA) in Quebec and the DNLA sped ahead with their efforts to educate the Indians, concentrating mainly on those they considered most open to new values and ideas.

Although the Canadian and New-foundland government focused most of their energies on assimilation, it did develop policies intended to bring aid to the Indians who were reluctant to learn English or French. The most important of these policies was aimed at helping the Innu maintain their annual hunting and trapping trips to the country. The DIA and the DNLA rented aircraft to transport men to their hunting and trapping grounds and arranged for food to be airlifted to them. But the government did not permit most of the Indian women and children to accompany the hunters, which was contrary to the Indians' traditional practices. The women and children were required to stay behind in their newly built government villages because school attendance was mandatory for all Innu children. Indeed, government officials in Quebec and Labrador threatened to stop the welfare payments and family allowance checks (funds to families with children) to families whose children were not sent to school. A Catholic scholar, John T. McGee, who studied

the Sheshatshit Innu in the early 1960s, commented on the situation:

> Compulsory school attendance may well become the chief factor conducive to a change of Montagnais outlook and culture. This is partly because through school the Indians are forced to learn English, which is certainly a means to their being employed locally above the menial level.

In the late 1950s and early 1960s, the Canadian government provided other incentives for the Innu to end their seasonal hunting expeditions. One of these was government housing. Another was wage employment, which both the Canadian and Newfoundland governments took steps to secure for the Indians. In central Labrador, Innu were employed to fight forest fires, explore uranium deposits, and work at the local hospital and mission. In 1961, the DIA started a commercial fishing operation in La Romaine, which employed about 50 Innu men for a 10- or 11-week period each summer. The fishery, which closed in 1973, was not successful because it was established at a time when prices for cod were at an all-time low and because the DIA provided only old and underpowered fishing boats. And in 1965, a sawmill was established by the Newfoundland government so that, in Paddon's words, "a start could be made in one way or another on the problem of making the Labrador Indian employable." It remained in operation for some years but closed down in 1982.

Many Innu eventually settled permanently in government-built villages. To some extent, government policies coerced them into making this decision. But the Indians were also in a sense "ready for settlement." For years, they had been weakened by disease, periodic starvation, and other physical deprivations. For many Innu, the security of village life, with its health care and housing facilities, appeared to be an attractive alternative to an increasingly difficult life on the land. Some Indians also believed that settlement was preferable because they wanted their children to learn English or French and to

receive a formal Canadian education. They hoped that these things would allow their children to be better able to deal with non-Indians and their governments.

But many Innu soon recognized that settlement was a tragic mistake. Alcohol abuse, family violence, and other terrible social problems became firmly entrenched in their communities—evidence of what some anthropologists call *culture collapse*. This problem occurs among the people native to an area when they lose effective control of their lives and access to their traditional lands. One symptom of culture collapse is the erosion of the people's self-es-

Innu houses in Sheshatshit in northern Labrador, photographed in 1977.

teem. As a result, their traditional worldview disintegrates, thus leaving them without the foundation upon which their values and the meaning of their lives were built. The victims of culture collapse often sink into despair and a sense of powerlessness as they come under pressure from immigrant populations and their governments. This, in turn, can lead to a downward spiral of self-hatred and increasingly self-destructive behavior.

George Henricksen, an anthropologist who worked among the Davis Inlet Innu between 1966 and 1968, observed the impact of settlement there. He maintains that alcohol abuse had become a serious problem among these Innu even prior to settlement. During the late 1950s, many Davis Inlet Innu camped at Sango Bay in the summer, living off government relief and drinking large amounts of homemade spruce beer. But when a new village was built at Davis Inlet in the late 1960s, alcohol abuse and other problems worsened. Immediately after settlement, life in the community was characterized by a growing dependence on government funds, an erosion of traditional values, family violence, and despair.

In Innu communities that bordered newly established Canadian settlements, such as Goose Bay, Schefferville, and Sept-Îles, the ill effects of culture collapse were reinforced by a constant barrage of messages from non-Indians that told the Innu that they were culturally inferior. The school system played a major role in giving Indian students a sense of inferiority. The racism of many of their non-Indian neighbors also lowered the Innu's self-esteem.

The experience of village life, with its humiliations, despair, and social problems, convinced many Innu in the eastern portion of Quebec-Labrador that they needed to revitalize their traditional hunting way of life. Therefore, in the mid-1970s, they decided to seek additional government funding for special "outpost" programs that would finance the cost of chartering planes to hunting camps far in the interior of Labrador and Quebec each fall and spring. The Indians recognized that a return to their traditions was a vital lifeline to their culture and their traditional religious practices. ▲

An Innu woman carrying spruce tree boughs back to her family's hunting camp. The branches will be used to line the floor of the family's tent.

REVITALIZING
A
CULTURE

Despite the ill effects of the Canadian government's Indian settlement policies, many eastern groups still spend several months of the year at hunting locations in the interior of the Quebec-Labrador peninsula. Here they harvest large and small game—such as fur-bearers, migratory waterfowl, and fish—as well as wild fruits and medicinal plants. Since the mid-1970s, the eastern Innu have traveled to the interior in an effort to maintain their traditional way of life.

Reviving their hunting culture has not proved simple, however, because so many Innu communities have lost access to much of their traditional hunting grounds. The Innu from Sheshatshit, Sept-Îles, and Schefferville have seen their hunting territory steadily reduced since the 1940s. The Innu have lost most of their lands because of industrial expansion. For example, Sheshatshit hunters suffered greatly after the construction of a massive hydroelectric facility and the creation of the Smallwood Reservoir at Churchill Falls. The reservoir inundated large areas of otherwise productive hunting territory as well as ancestral grave sites and an area long used as a meeting place by Indians from throughout eastern Quebec-Labrador. According to one hunter from Sheshatshit:

Our hunting territory is no good to us anymore, because all our traps and belongings are under water. We lost mostly Indian-made items. I lost two canoes, about 500 traps, snowshoes, caribou-hide scrapers, beaming tools, ice chisels, axes, and many other items. We knew that there was going to be damming of the river, but we did not know what it would mean. We had no idea of what the level of the water would be. At most, we compared it to a beaver damming a river.

Innu now living in the villages of Sept-Îles, Maliotenam, and Schefferville lost access to hunting lands when iron ore mines were built at Wabush and Labrador City in western Labrador in the 1950s. Their economic problems were greatly compounded by the near extermination of the Lake Joseph caribou herd, the population of which declined in that decade to fewer than 200 head. Luckily, the Innu of Sept-Îles and Maliotenam have been able to hunt the massive George River caribou herd near Schefferville and have thereby been able to obtain a stable supply of meat, hides, and sacred bone marrow.

Likewise, the Sheshatshit Innu have been hurt by a substantial decline in the population of the Mealy Mountain caribou herd, which included fewer than 300 head in the 1960s. As a result, the Newfoundland government imposed a ban on all caribou hunting in the Mealy Mountains. Biologist Arthur Bergerud has attributed the reduction in the size of the herd to overhunting by non-Innu from Happy Valley/Goose Bay and Cartwright in 1958 and 1959. The Indians were therefore denied access to one of their most important food sources because of actions by non-Indian hunters.

The Newfoundland government in general does not recognize the hunting rights of the Innu. Over the past 15 years, it has prosecuted numerous Indians from Sheshatshit, St. Augustin, La Romaine, Sept-Îles, Maliotenam, and Schefferville for violating federal and provincial hunting regulations, which include bans on hunting Mealy Mountain and Lake Joseph caribou. Some Innu hunters have been heavily penalized. In one case, 6 men were fined $500 each and forbidden to hunt big game for 5 years because they killed Mealy Mountain caribou.

For the most part, the Innu have continued to hunt in Labrador despite government officials' constant searches of their campsites and their homes. In Sheshatshit, Indians have had their meat, rifles, traps, and snowmobiles confiscated as well as being fined and given prison sentences. The Innu hunters continue to practice their traditions despite this harassment because they believe it is their right. They have never signed away their territory in a treaty with the Canadian government. Therefore, they feel that they are not subject to federal regulations and believe that the Quebec-Labrador peninsula is still theirs.

Preparations for the fall hunting season begins in early August. During that time, men from settlements at Sheshatshit, Utshimassit, St. Augustin, La Romaine, Natashquan, Mingan, and Schefferville visit one another to finalize decisions about where they will establish camps during the upcoming season. The Indians also begin to gather their traps and other hunting supplies. Then they purchase canvas from the Hudson's Bay Company or the provincial government store that they will use to make new tents. Advances on welfare payments are requested from the Canadian government's Department of

(continued on page 65)

ROBES
OF
POWER
AND
BEAUTY

Until recently, little has been known about the origin and meaning of the Innu's beautifully crafted caribou-hide robes, or mishtikuai. Only since the 1960s have anthropologists begun to understand the role the robes played in the Innu's hunting rituals.

According to anthropologist Alicia Podolinsky Webber, Innu spiritual leaders, or shamans, wore decorated robes during many ceremonial rites, most importantly the makushan (ritual caribou feast), as well as during ceremonies prior to the hunt. When the Innu embarked on a caribou hunt, they looked to a shaman for guidance. By wrapping his body in his caribou robe, the shaman could magically transform himself into a caribou, which allowed him to attract more of his kind. When a herd came close enough to be ambushed by the young hunters, the shaman would remove his robe, transforming himself back into a man.

Less powerful individuals also wore caribou hides. These hides were usually made into coats that were decorated with paints and worn during hunting trips.

Most ceremonial robes and coats were decorated with simple patterns painted with a bone tool. The size and detail of the designs used indicated the amount of spiritual power possessed by each garment. Shamans' robes were always the most intricately patterned. Only with his son would a shaman share the secret significance of these designs.

By the 1960s, use of the ceremonial hunting garments had all but vanished among the Innu. Luckily, the artifacts survive, providing insight into traditional Innu life.

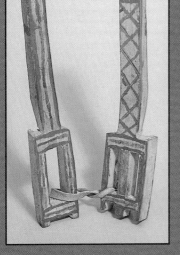

Bone tools such as these were used by shamans' wives to paint line designs on caribou-skin robes.

The front and back of a child's caribou skin coat. The dotted motifs were probably made with a quill pen.

Line designs such as those adorning this coat often represented tracks of game, of a toboggan loaded with meat, or a path leading to caribou.

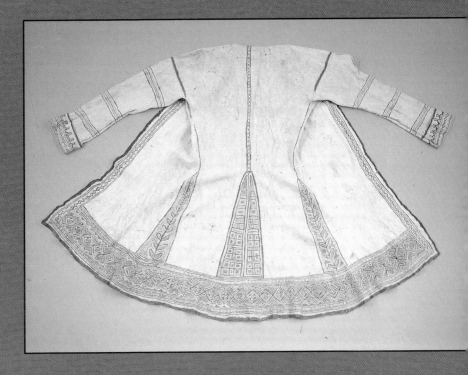

Innu hunters often wrapped themselves in special hide coats while stalking caribou. These were worn with the painted design turned inside in order to protect the power, which would be readily absorbed by the wearer. When a hunter killed an animal, he removed his coat immediately and stored it away in a special bag, because the Innu believed that the taint of caribou blood would greatly reduce the spiritual power of the skin.

A back view of an elaborately decorated woman's outer dress.

A front and back view of a robe with a fringed hood. The hood allowed the shaman to envelope his face in darkness, a state in which he would sit for hours waiting for a vision, helping him guide his people to caribou.

The small painted discs on this summer robe may represent the sun. The discs would be larger on coats worn in cooler months, in order to encourage the spirits to send good weather.

The elaborate detail of this coat suggests it was worn by a powerful Innu shaman.

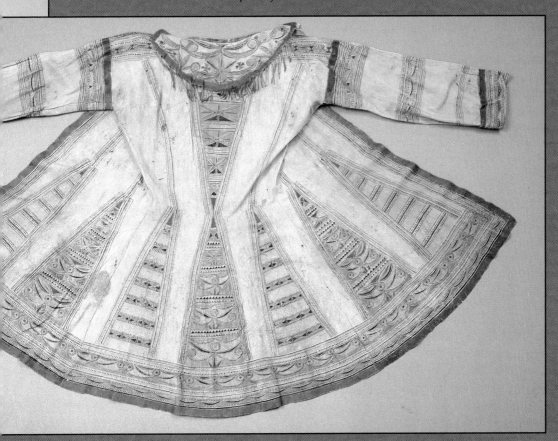

This robe, which may date from as early as 1740, is edged in fringe. It was originally bound with red zigzag quillwork of which only fragments now remain. The painted designs on the piece were created with fish glue, which has yellowed with age, giving the robe its gold tone.

(continued from page 56)
Social Services so that families will have the money to purchase flour, tea, sugar, lard, baking powder, beans, potatoes, ammunition, and other supplies. In this manner, the Innu slowly accumulate all the provisions required for their stay in the country.

In late August or early September, each band council (the decision-making body in Innu settlements) makes arrangements to charter small aircraft, using funds from the Canadian govern-ment's Outpost and Trapping Pro-gramme. The planes will transport families to their camps in the Quebec-Labrador interior. There is no set date for their departure. Many factors, such as weather conditions, determine when the planes will take off. But there is always an air of excitement and expectation in Innu communities at this time. The members of each group look forward to relief from the boredom and the social problems of life in their govern-

A group of caribou in the Quebec-Labrador interior.

ment-built settlements. They are also eager for the traditional foods, such as ducks, geese, lake trout, spruce grouse, beavers, and muskrat. If the hunt is very successful, the Indians may bring back caribou. Once again, the Innu will be engaged in activities that have meaning to them and give them great satisfaction.

Few non-Indian people can fully appreciate the importance to the Innu of their traditional hunting country and hunting economy. Many Innu feel truly at home only in the country. The hunting territories provide a meaningful context in which the Innu perform their daily tasks, such as walking or canoeing for many miles and gathering firewood and fir boughs.

The first person to arrive at the fall hunting encampment is the *utshimau*, or hunting group leader. He is usually a middle-aged man who knows the area and is responsible for spiritual and managerial guidance of the season's hunting. The rest of the hunting party soon follows and sets up camp on the shore of a lake large enough for float planes to land and take off. The hunters usually choose a campsite on the northern edge of the lake so that they will be sheltered from the wind and so that they have a commanding view of the area. This allows them to easily spot swimming or wading animals, such as muskrat, waterfowl, and even caribou. The Indians also seek a body of water in which to set their fishnets in order to catch brook trout, lake trout, whitefish, and northern pike. The availability

of fir boughs for making tent floors and deadwood for use as fuel is another important consideration in choosing a campsite.

Camps usually consist of from two to eight tents. Innu families construct them using wooden poles cut from nearby trees and then cover them with sheets of canvas. Each dwelling is equipped with a rectangular sheet-metal stove with a pipe that sticks up through the roof or front wall of the tent. The families keep their personal possessions, their food supplies, and all of their bedding in the tent throughout the hunting season.

A typical day in an Innu hunting camp begins at four or five o'clock in the morning. The elder members of the group take care of the first task of the morning—checking the nets. If they contain fish, the younger members of the camp wake to the smell of fish frying on the tent stoves. Breakfast commonly consists of bannock (unleavened bread), strong tea, porridge, fried fish, and muskrat or beaver stew.

After breakfast, Innu women begin their daily tasks, such as caring for the children, gathering fir boughs for the tent floor, cooking meals, cutting firewood, and preparing the furs of the captured game. In addition, the women also engage in a number of harvesting activities, including gathering berries, setting snares for hares, hunting small game, and fishing. Occasionally, women accompany their husbands on short hunting trips. Older women often spend their time in the camps making

Innu families preparing to board planes that will take them to their hunting sites, photographed in 1982.

goods, such as snowshoes, moccasins, mittens, and socks.

Soon after breakfast, the men quickly make preparations to leave camp for the day's work of hunting and checking traps. After sunrise, they load their supplies, game bags, axes, and rifles into canoes if they are traveling by water. If they are traveling by foot, they carry their implements in hand and throw their hunting sacks over their shoulders.

Innu men hunt for a wide variety of game. They usually take whatever animals they find. These often include spruce grouse, muskrat, geese, ducks,

A 1982 photograph of Helen Mark cleaning a beaver skin in her family's tent.

An Innu woman lacing snowshoes. This traditional method of travel is still one of the best ways to get around during the snowy winters of Quebec and Labrador.

loons, and owls. They also trap a variety of fur-bearing animals, such as beavers, marten, mink, weasels, otters, and foxes. Hunting and trapping are not performed independently of each other, however. Innu hunters may rapidly shift their attention from one of these tasks to the other, depending on circumstances. In this regard, the Innu have much in common with other Indian peoples in the subarctic regions of North America. In their often harsh environment, northern hunting societies must maintain a flexible system of food collection—one that takes advantage of all available food resources.

Innu hunters usually set off on a predetermined course, but their plans are always flexible enough to accommodate changes. These Indian hunters do not view planning in the same way that non-Indian North Americans do. They always take into account the constant shifts in nature, in the spirit world, and in human moods. For example, an Innu hunting party may intend to spend one morning checking traps, but if they come upon some game

Innu hunters often walk great distances each day during their expeditions into the forest.

animals they may choose to hunt the animals first and attend to their traps later. Or they may spot caribou tracks on the shore and abandon their trapping plans altogether in order to spend the day hunting.

The Innu usually check their traps every three to five days. However, this varies with changes in weather conditions and hunting plans. Animal traps must be visited frequently because there is always a risk of having a trap-

ped animal escape, losing it to a predator, or having the traps set off by mice or birds.

At the end of each day, the sound of laughter and conversation can be heard as camp members share information about the movement of game, their recent hunting successes, fur prices, ice conditions, the weather, the arrival of bush planes, and other topics on their two-way portable radios. These are an invaluable means of quickly passing information among camps and are used for a variety of purposes. These include calling for help during medical emergencies and listening to the Catholic religious service that is performed every Sunday, a day of rest and relaxation in the hunting camps. At the conclusion of this service, a representative from each camp offers a word of thanks on behalf of the camp members, such as "Tshinashkumitan Nitshukunipi," or "thank you from Otter Lake."

The Innu's hunting activities change throughout the months they spend in the country. For example, they hunt ducks and geese only until the middle of October, at which time the birds migrate farther to the south. Loons also fly south during the third week of October as the lakes begin to freeze. At this time, the Innu pull up their fishnets and wait for the ice to become thick enough so that they can walk on it. Then women and children catch fish by chopping holes in the ice and dropping lines with baited hooks into them.

Innu women and children hunt for small game throughout the fall. But they confine their redberry gathering to September and early October in locations well known for their abundance of this wild fruit. Redberries are also a favorite food of the black bear, so these animals are likely to be found wherever the berries are ripe. Innu hunters take full advantage of this situation and usually kill at least one of these bears each season.

At the end of the fall hunting season, the Innu make preparations to return to their government villages. The hunters visit the traps one last time and then take them back to camp. There they either pack the traps for transport back to their village or store them at the campsite. A final round of small game hunting is usually undertaken as well. Then, using their two-way radios, the Innu make arrangements for a plane to pick them up and take them back to

Innu Francois Bellefleur from La Romaine contacting other families at his hunting site by means of his short-wave radio.

their villages. This sparks a new kind of excitement and expectation among the people. After three or four months of separation from friends and relatives, the hunting parties eagerly anticipate a Christmas reunion.

Many hunting parties return to the villages in early December, at which time the men join caribou-hunting parties traveling into the interior by aircraft or by snowmobile. For example, the Indians at Davis Inlet, an island community, travel over the frozen sea to the mainland of Labrador. Here they have ready access to the barren grounds where caribou herds sometimes come to feed. The men from the Innu communities at Schefferville and along the Quebec North Shore also take part in caribou hunts, which often last for 1 or 2 weeks and may take them more than 100 miles away. Men from Sept-Îles and Maliotenam often take the train to Schefferville to join in these hunts.

Almost all of the Innu hunting parties return to their community by December 23 in order to celebrate Christmas. At this time, parents spend time purchasing gifts for their children, and women prepare a variety of foods

A home in Davis Inlet. On the roof are boxes of caribou meat and bones that will be used in a makushan *feast. The Indians store the food atop their houses to keep it out of the reach of animals and children.*

A group of men and boys from Davis Inlet repairing a snowmobile. The Innu must keep these vehicles in working order at all costs because they are an important means of long-distance transportation during the winter.

for the holiday season. Many community members put up Christmas trees, as well. When caribou are on hand, the Indians participate in a feast known as *makushan*. In preparation for the festival, caribou leg bones, meat, and hides are piled in boxes on top of the village houses, out of the reach of the dogs and children. Then, for a day or more prior to the feast, one can hear the methodical pounding of the leg bones going on inside the houses as the raw marrow is extracted from the bones.

Aside from caribou-hunting trips, the Innu perform few animal-harvesting tasks in January and February. They instead spend time socializing, caring for their children, and restocking their supplies of firewood. The extremely cold weather during these months makes lengthy travel out-of-doors uncomfortable. However, a few men con-

Two Innu men and their daughters from La Romaine relaxing after a day of gathering food resources.

tinue to trap marten, foxes, mink, and wolves and to catch fish with nets dropped through the ice. The hunters in the northern Innu communities, such as Davis Inlet, continue to hunt caribou even in the coldest months.

During March and April, caribou-hunting parties from Davis Inlet, Sept-Îles, Maliotenam, Schefferville, and Kawawachikamach travel into caribou grounds in the northern interior of Labrador and Quebec. The groups, which usually consist of up to 10 men, travel by snowmobile across the frozen landscape. This method of hunting becomes increasingly dangerous because the snow melts as the temperature rises. Occasionally, hunting parties get stranded on the barrens if an unex-

pected warm spell causes ice on the rivers to break up, making them impassable. Furthermore, the soft snow conditions and warm temperatures place an added strain on the snowmobiles and make it difficult to haul heavy loads of caribou meat. In order to avoid these problems, hunters often wait until early morning to travel because the river and lake surfaces have usually refrozen during the night.

In the spring, Innu hunters display their skill as expert mechanics, using whatever materials they have at hand to keep their heavily used snowmobiles in working order. These machines are very important to the Indians because they allow them to exploit a wide and varied range of hunting territory. They are thus able to hunt many types of migratory waterfowl and fish for trout and other species of fish. Sometimes entire families establish camps near local waterways for periods ranging from one to four weeks. Hunters travel by snowmobile out onto sea ice in May to hunt seals and into the interior during March, April, and May to hunt porcupines.

For the Sheshatshit Innu who go to the country in the spring, harvesting activities in many respects mirror those of the previous autumn. They set their traps for furbearers, hunt for food animals, fish in the lakes, and harvest berries and other wild fruits. These activities continue only until late June, by which time many animals have migrated out of range and black flies have begun to swarm. Travel by snowmobile also becomes impossible at this time.

The spring hunting parties return to their villages in late June. At this time Sheshatshit men sometimes join short-term hunting parties to harvest sea gull eggs or to hunt seabirds such as puffins at the eastern end of Lake Melville. Innu on the Quebec North Shore fish for trout, hunt for ducks and geese, and trap lobsters throughout the late spring. For instance, in La Romaine, the Innu devote a great deal of time to catching lobsters and fish during the month of June. These shellfish, in great abundance in the shallow waters around the La Romaine community, are a cherished delicacy.

During the summer, Davis Inlet and Quebec North Shore hunters continue to harvest ducks and geese along the coast and in the vicinity of the islands near the community. The summer months are a time for harvesting young sea gulls and gathering bird eggs and wild fruits. The men also hunt seals and fish for trout, arctic char, and salmon from boats. At Davis Inlet, the men hunt a few caribou at various locations along the coast and up river valleys that are accessible by boat. The women gather sea gull eggs, catch fish, and care for children. In La Romaine, July and August are important months for canoe making. More than 20 of these canvas-and-wood craft, which are modeled on the traditional birchbark style, may be made each summer.

With the approach of September, the yearly cycle of Innu harvesting activities comes full circle. They again turn their attention to their preparations for traveling back out to the country. Welfare advances are requested, provisions and new equipment are purchased, transportation arrangements are made, and the composition of the fall hunting groups is finalized. After all these tasks are completed, groups of hunters once more set out to experience the way of life that has long given their people their identity as Innu. ▲

An Innu drummer, photographed in the early 20th century. Ritual drumming was a means of divination, or foretelling the future, and could be performed only by those people who had acquired sufficient spiritual power.

OLD AND
NEW BELIEFS

More than 400 years of contact with Europeans have changed the religious practices of the Innu to some degree. Many are now devout Catholics. However, their traditional religion, which is inseparable from their hunting way of life, has proved surprisingly resistant to change. It has persisted until the present day in many communities. In fact, most of the beliefs presently held by the Innu are almost identical to those recorded by the first Christian missionaries who came to work among them during the 17th century.

One probable reason for the survival of the Innu's beliefs and practices is that they see no contradiction between belief in God and Jesus and belief in their own traditional deities—the animal masters and forest spirits. God is responsible for overseeing the activities of human beings, and the animal masters watch over the activities of animals and their treatment by human beings.

The Innu possess an elaborate naming system that divides animals into different categories. They first designate all animals as being either European or Indian. The Indian animals are further divided into five categories—four-legged animals, waterfowl, birds, fish, and insects. The various animal species also belong to *tipentamuna*, or kingdoms. Each tipentamun is governed by an animal spirit called *utshimau* (chief or master), *aueshish-utshimau* (master of the animals), or *katipenitak* (controller).

Some Innu groups believe that certain animal masters are more powerful than others. For example, the La Romaine people believe that Papakasht-shihk, the caribou spirit who lives in the Ungava Bay region in a house filled with animals and their masters, controls all of these individual animal masters. An Innu hunter has recently tried to explain the relationship between the caribou boss and the other spirits by comparing it to the relationship between Canada's prime minister and his cabinet ministers.

The Innu believe that both their spiritual and material well-being are dependent upon maintaining good relations with the animal masters. It is the animal masters who allow the hunters to kill game and provide food for their family. Animals cannot be hunted without the animal master's cooperation. In order to gain the animal masters' favor, a hunter must show them respect by following certain rules. These include keeping the bones of hunted animals from harm, placing animal fat and leftovers in the fire, and wearing decorated clothing while hunting. Anthropologist George Henricksen has noted:

> A hunter does not kill an animal against its will, but with its consent. Hunters and hunted are alike part of nature. As long as . . . [they] follow the customs of their people, as handed down from their forefathers, and they do not offend the animals and their spiritual masters, they will continue to live in peace with each other and with nature.

The Innu believe that it is important to keep the bones and other remains of game animals together and dispose of them properly. This is because the an-

A caribou hide painted with designs that symbolize the tracks and location of game animals.

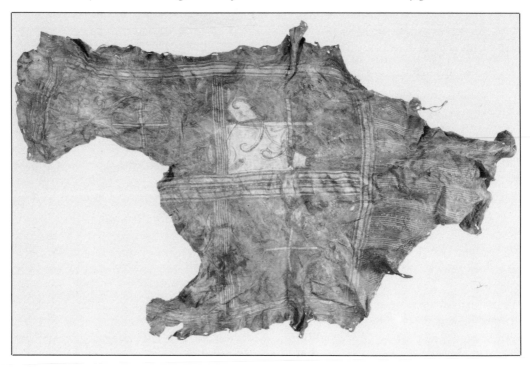

imal masters need them to create new animals. If the Indians fail to follow these and other rules, the animal masters will become angry and punish the offending persons. Punished individuals are usually refused the opportunity to kill any more animals. In other words, the guilty person will have no success in future attempts to hunt the species whose animal master he has offended.

A Sheshatshit hunter has explained the nature of the Innu's relationship with the animal masters by making this analogy:

> The animal masters give you credit. The credit is an allocation of the animals under their control for the next year. If you show proper respect to the animals that year, your line of credit will be extended into the following year. However, if you show disrespect, you will lose your credit and have no success in hunting the following year.

The hunter had himself once offended the master of mink by not checking his traps regularly. As a result, a trapped mink had been partly devoured by another animal. The man felt that the animal master's anger with him over this incident explained his subsequent failure to trap mink.

The distribution of game among the village residents is also regulated by the laws of the animal spirits. These laws dictate that when a hunting party returns to the camp or to the community, the game is distributed to relatives and

A hunter from the Eastern Cree settlement at Mistassini engaging in scapulimancy, *in which the scapula, or shoulder bone, of a caribou, porcupine, or hare is burned and then used as a map to locate game.*

friends by the hunter's wife or mother. It is first given to close relatives, such as parents, siblings, children, and especially grandparents. If there is any meat left over, it is offered to more distant kin and finally to close friends and neighbors. In theory, however, the harvest should be shared with anyone who asks for food.

The animal masters provide the Innu with invaluable information about the world around them as well as about the world of the spirits. However, the Indians cannot speak with the animal masters directly. They must employ

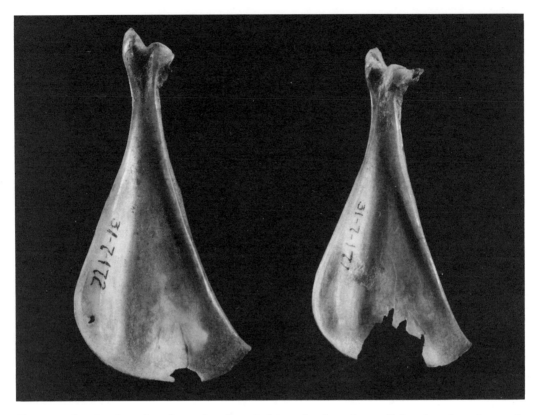

Two scapulae that have been burned and cracked in a fire in order to divine the whereabouts of animal resources.

several methods of divination (a magical procedure by which the cause of an event may be determined or the future foretold), including ritual drumming and dream analysis.

Not everyone can communicate with the spirits by playing the drum. The task is reserved for older men who have dreamed about drumming on three previous occasions. A drummer plays and sings ritual songs until he falls into a trance in which he sees "sparks" on the drum's skin. The size of these sparks and their location on the drumhead indicate the number of caribou that may be killed by a group of hunters and the animal's approximate location in relation to the hunting camp.

A further means of communication with the world of the animal masters is the analysis of *puamuna*, or dreams. Many Innu people believe that their puamuna are messages from the animal masters. For one 35-year-old hunter based in Sheshatshit, dreams provided clues to future hunting successes and reasons for failure in the past. He explained:

> Once I dreamt about a lynx woman coming toward me. She was extremely beautiful. Just as I was about to take her hand, my brother came and took her from me. That fall, my brother killed lynx while I killed none.

The Innu believe that when certain items, animals, or people appear in their dreams, these things refer to specific events in the future. For example, if a hunter dreams about a woman, it means that he will soon kill many animals. If a woman dreams about a man, this also means she will have good luck at hunting in the near future. A dream in which a man or woman is angry, however, signifies coming bad luck in the hunt. Dreaming about a check is good because it means a hunter will soon kill many "money animals," that is, furbearers whose pelts can be sold for cash. The arrival of an aircraft in the dream indicates that a visitor may soon arrive at the camp.

Another method of divination used by the Innu is known as *scapulimancy*, which the Innu call *matinikashauew*. The root of the word is *scapula*, the Latin term for "shoulder blade." To use this method of foretelling the future, an elderly Innu man holds the shoulder blade of a porcupine or caribou over the flame from a stove or candle until it is charred and cracked. The scorch marks and cracks are then studied like a map to determine the possible location of game.

One of the most important divination rituals in traditional Innu society was the shaking-tent ceremony, which was called *kushapatshikan* in the Innu-aimun language. The shaking tent was a small, conical structure with a framework of between four and eight poles and a caribou-hide covering. In summer, it was erected in the open air. During winter, however, it was set up

Innu elder and author Mathieu André, photographed in 1989. He is among the group of Innu leaders actively seeking to teach younger Innu about their traditions.

A 1928 photograph of an Innu hunter preparing caribou bones for makushan.

inside another tent on a floor of freshly picked fir boughs.

The shaking-tent ceremony was performed by the village shaman, or religious leader, known as a *kamanitushit*. In the tent, he looked into the hidden world of animal spirits and made contact with people in distant groups. Occasionally, he brought the souls of people living in other groups into the tent or waged terrible battles there with other shamans or cannibal spirits.

Innu elder and author Mathieu André described what he saw during the ceremony, which he witnessed as a young man:

The ritual must take place in the darkness, because the shaman is looking for the light in the animal [masters'] eyes. As soon as the shaman enters the tent, it starts to shake, the poles bend and flatten on all sides. A whistling sound like a strong wind in the trees can be heard.

Then the buzzing of black flies is heard, and they attack the tent. Once inside, the flies hurl themselves against the walls. They are said to be the spirits of the animals the shaman has killed. The sounds of animals can then be heard, the cries of caribou, geese, [and other birds]. You really have the impression you're on a duck hunt.

Next, someone is heard speaking inside the tent, what we call "kainnuaimit," or one who speaks Montagnais or "mishtapeu." He acts as interpreter for the animals, the shaman, and the people asking the questions. Everyone takes part in the rite: children, adults, elders. It lasts several hours.

According to the Innu, the shaking tent was a very powerful but dangerous device. It could kill people who entered it unless they had accumulated substantial spiritual power. Such power could be gained only through hunting. A hunter obtained some spiritual power each time he killed an animal. An Innu woman could not conduct the shaking-tent ritual, but she could assist her husband in the ceremony. A woman acquired spiritual power by butchering, cooking, and preparing the hides of the animals that were killed by her husband and other relatives. However, it was not as great as that of the hunters.

The Innu were still performing the shaking-tent ceremony well into the 20th century. Despite the best efforts of the Catholic church to eradicate the ritual, it persisted up until about 1957 among the Davis Inlet Indians and until about 1973 among the Innu at Sheshatshit. The ritual eventually disappeared because of several factors, including less time being spent on traditional lands.

The Innu have a rich oral tradition that includes countless stories. These are generally divided into two categories. The first type, *tipatshamuna*, are historical accounts of the real-life events of Innu people, their travels in the country, and their dealings with spirits, other peoples, the Hudson's Bay Company, the church, and the Canadian government. The second category of tales, *atanukana*, contain myths about the creation of the world and about a time long ago when mythical beings underwent transformations between human and animal states. In one such myth, called the *Kanipinikassikueu*, the Caribou Man goes to live with the caribou, marries a female member of the herd, and is transformed into a caribou himself. He then becomes the caribou animal master. Some of these myths occur in Tshishtashkamuk, the land of Mishtapeu; others occur on the earth itself. As a whole, these tales generally reflect the very basic human need to understand the world, including nature and human society.

The Innu myth of the origin of the world is the *Kuekuatsheu*. In this tale, Kuekuatsheu (the wolverine) creates the world and everything in it. The wolverine hero is portrayed as an intelligent but sometimes foolish trickster. Kuekuatsheu is similar to the trickster characters found in the myths of many other Native American peoples, including the Cree, Ojibwa, Assiniboin, Winnebago, and Tlingit. Anthropologist Paul Radin's description of the typical trickster figure clearly applies to the Innu's Kuekuatsheu:

> Trickster is at one and the same time creator and destroyer, giver and negator, he who [fools] others and who is always [fooled] himself. He knows neither good nor evil yet he is responsible for both. He possesses no values, moral or social, is at the mercy of his passions and appetites, yet through his actions all values come into being.

One of the most important traditional rituals in Innu society is the makushan feast, which continues to play an important role in a number of Innu communities. The ceremony begins with the crushing and boiling of caribou leg bones. This process is supervised by a *utshimau-ushkan*, or "first man of the long bones." When the meal is ready for consumption, a *menatshitsh makushan* (he who looks well after makushan) takes over the supervisory role. He makes sure that proper disposal and other feast rules are followed. These include a requirement that most of the caribou bone marrow, cakes of caribou fat called *atiku-pimi*, and caribou meat be eaten indoors. Another law requires that none of the caribou be given to dogs. In fact, one of the worst calamities to befall the Innu at a feast would be for a dog to consume any part of a caribou.

During makushan, the oldest men eat first, then the other men, then the women, and finally the children. On some occasions, a dance is held after the feast during which an older man drums and sings quietly in a subdued, candle-lit corner of a tent or house. Community members of both sexes and all ages then dance in a clockwise circle in the center of the dwelling, all the while laughing and offering each other encouragement. The entire ritual, which includes eating, dancing, card

A ceremonial string that was traditionally used to haul game back to camp.

playing, and other relaxed activities, can last as long as 12 hours. At the conclusion of the feast, all the participants must wipe their mouth and plate scrupulously clean with a cloth and throw it into the stove to pay respect to the animal masters.

Makushan is not the only occasion on which the Innu show great respect for their elders. Older people are accorded a special status at all times. One example of this is the way in which community members refer to people older than themselves. For example, a young person must not call an elder by his or her personal name. Instead, he or she must call that person *nukum* (my grandmother) or *nimushum* (my grandfather).

The privileged position of the elderly among the Innu is also evidenced in the distribution of food. Great emphasis is placed on providing the elderly with a steady supply of meat, often the choicest morsels. Special portions of game animals are reserved for the consumption of the elderly alone. For example, the elders are given caribou fetuses and bear paws.

The reverence with which the Innu treat their elders is due in large part to the elders' perceived ability to communicate effectively with the animal masters and other spirit beings. The elders play an important role in the Indians' relations with the animal masters, and they help to defend the younger community members from attacks by hostile shamans and spirits. Many Innu believe that elders are able to combat dangerous shamans and unfriendly beings in their dreams.

Such powers were recently exercised by a shaman in the Innu community of Davis Inlet. This man, the son of a powerful religious leader, was greatly respected, and perhaps feared, by the members of his community. In 1985, political leaders from Sheshatshit visited Davis Inlet. One of them began to fight with a close relative of the shaman's. In retaliation, the shaman promised to curse the plane transporting the Sheshatshit men back to Goose Bay and cause it to crash. Soon afterward, a plane that belonged to the Regional Health Association crashed, and all but three of its passengers were killed. The residents of Davis Inlet believed that the shaman's curse had been successful but had struck the wrong target. The community members thought that the shaman had also been responsible for an earlier car accident in Schefferville in which a number of people were injured. When the shaman died suddenly in 1986 from no apparent cause, the members of his community speculated that he himself had been the victim of a curse made by a vengeful shaman from Schefferville.

The elder shaman's stature in the community was displayed during his funeral. Immediately after his death, all the lights were turned on in his house, and his clothing, hunting equipment, and other personal items were hung up outside in the trees. A curfew was then imposed on the village forbidding anyone to leave home after dark. On the

A ritual pipe used to bring luck in the hunt. An Innu hunter would smoke a pipe such as this one as an offering to the spirits of dead animals so that they would not prevent him from capturing game.

day of the shaman's burial, virtually every man, woman, and child joined the funeral procession and accompanied the corpse to the grave.

The esteemed position of shamans and elders, the myths, the ceremonies, and the reverence with which hunted animals are treated all speak of the richness of the Innu's hunting culture. It is not surprising, therefore, that the Indians chose to actively revive it in the hope of combating non-Indian threats to their identity. Hunting seasons in the interior have given the Innu a new feeling of hope for the future. ▲

Innu youngster Jack Penashua peers from inside his family's tent at their hunting camp.

NEW
CHALLENGES

The Innu face major challenges in the near future. In many communities, there are serious problems, such as alcohol abuse, depression, and child abuse, that threaten the survival of the people and their culture. Many Indian people, particularly young adults, are injured or die each year because of alcohol-related accidents and illnesses. For example, one man from Sheshatshit reported that alcohol abuse caused the death of his parents, his brother, his sister-in-law, and his brother-in-law. Innu children of alcoholic parents are often not fed properly and not sent to school. As a result, the Newfoundland or Quebec Department of Social Services must remove these children from their homes and place them in a village group home or in foster care.

Young people are subject to the greatest difficulties in the Indians' rapidly changing world. Many of them suffer from identity crises as they attempt to combine their traditional hunting way of life with the values and practices of mainstream Canadian life that they encounter at school and on television. For example, during 1988, 21 young people in Sheshatshit attempted suicide. Some Indian adolescents have also become drug users as well as alcoholics.

Many younger people are also beginning to show a declining interest in hunting and trapping. Innu adolescents are constantly exposed to the values of industrial Canadian society and, as a result, place less value on traditional activities. They often prefer to find jobs when possible or simply maintain an existence that is totally dependent on social security.

The serious social problems that plague many Innu communities may well worsen in the future as the younger generations mature. More than half of the people in most communities are under 20 years of age. Furthermore, there are currently only a few people more than 65 years of age. These

Uipit Bellefleur and his grandson at their hunting camp north of La Romaine. During the last decade, the gap between generations has widened among the Innu. Young people have been increasingly exposed to mainstream Canadian values and practices, often at the expense of their traditions.

people are the repositories of invaluable knowledge about the land, animals, religion, and other aspects of traditional Innu culture. If they die without passing on this knowledge, it will be lost forever.

For the Innu, the most important time for exchanging traditional knowledge is during the seasonal hunting expeditions to the Quebec-Labrador interior. The country is the most appropriate setting for contact between the generations. But industrial development in the interior Quebec-Labrador peninsula could well jeopardize this important practice. In fact, massive industrial activities are now on the horizon for Innu territory. The provincial governments of Quebec and Newfoundland are planning several large hydroelectric complexes on major waterways on the Quebec North Shore and along the lower Churchill River. These developments will flood large areas of the Indians' most productive hunting and trapping territory. Also under construction is a new roadway, called the Trans-Labrador Highway, that will connect Labrador City, Happy Valley/Goose Bay, and Churchill Falls and link these northern settlements to Montreal and to the rest of North America. The Trans-Labrador Highway— non-Indians in Labrador have nicknamed it the "freedom road"—will open up large tracts of land to mining, logging, and other destructive industries. The highway will also allow thousands of tourists to enter the region each year. Many of them will compete with the Innu for access to the region's increasingly scarce wildlife resources.

Another threat to the Innu's hunting territory is a proposed military flight training installation. It will be constructed in northern Labrador under the direction of the North Atlantic Treaty Organization (NATO), a military alliance between several Western nations, including Canada, the United States, and Great Britain. Goose Bay in

Labrador has been chosen as the site for a new massive military installation known as the Tactical Fighter and Weapons Training Centre. The facility will provide pilots with training in the techniques of modern air warfare. Much of the hunting territories of the Sheshatshit, Davis Inlet, La Romaine, and Natashquan Indians are located in these special flight training zones.

Military jets, including extremely loud supersonic models, have frequently flown over Indian camps and hunting parties. The Innu fear that more bombing ranges (nine have been proposed), low-flying-jet noise, and sonic booms will render much of their territory uninhabitable and make life on the land impossible for them. The Indians report that the noise produced by jets has seriously traumatized their children and elders and may have a harmful effect on the wildlife. Such military operations have previously provoked vigorous protests from the Innu, resulting in numerous arrests.

One thing is clear. Canada will not abandon its efforts to promote industrial and military development of Innu land. One option available to the Indians is the negotiation of land-claims agreements with the Canadian govern-

An aerial view of a hydroelectric installation in northern Quebec. In the near future, the Quebec and Newfoundland governments will construct several of these dams on Innu land, thus flooding large portions of the Indians' most productive hunting territory.

ment. Unlike Indian groups to the west, such as the Déné, the Nishga, and the Inuit, virtually none of the Innu groups has ever signed a treaty in which it gave up rights to land. The only exception to this are the people of Kawawachika-mach, who in 1978 signed a land-claims agreement (the modern version of the 18th- and 19th-century treaties).

In 1973, the Canadian government instituted a new set of guidelines for native land claims that would allow un-impeded resource development and non-Indian settlement in the north. The policy, which is still in effect, requires native peoples to give up all rights to their traditional lands in return for a variety of rights and benefits. These in-clude special rights to hunt, trap, and fish on former native homelands, active Indian participation in wildlife manage-ment, subsurface mineral rights, mon-etary compensation, control over education and health care, and some degree of self-government.

In response to these government ac-tions, a new political awareness has emerged among the native peoples of Canada. Several organizations have been formed in order to negotiate land-claims agreements with the Canadian federal and provincial governments. However, the Canadian government will only deal with six groups at a time. The Innu representatives, the Conseil Attikamek-Montagnais (CAM, formed

Daniel Ashini, leader of the Innu community at Sheshatshit, speaks to a reporter during a demonstration protesting low-level jet flights over Innu hunting land.

Several Innu delegates, including CAM (Conseil Attikamek-Montagnais, the Innu negotiating body) spokesperson Bernard Cleary, meeting with Quebec government officials and representatives from various industries at the 1988 Sept-Îles regional forum. During the meeting, the Innu submitted proposals for 15 projects aimed at improving their economy and the social services in their communities.

in 1975), will negotiate for three Attikamek and nine Innu communities in Quebec. CAM is currently engaged in negotiations with the Canadian government and has signed an agreement that is supposed to protect their lands from development during the meetings.

In its program to establish Innu rights, CAM stressed several important issues. These included self-determinaion and sovereignty in their homeland, a refusal to turn over any territory to the government as a prerequisite of land-claims agreements, and compensation for federal and provincial violations of the Indians' territorial rights.

They also opposed any new projects that would exploit the resources in their territories until their rights are recognized. CAM demanded that the Indians be given the right to choose which resources are exploited and to control industrial plans. As CAM representatives noted, "We want to orient development to the values and traditions bequeathed by our ancestors and which were developed during thousands of years of harmony with our natural and social environments."

The Labrador Indians are represented by an organization called the Naskapi Montagnais Innu Association

INNU SETTLEMENTS TODAY

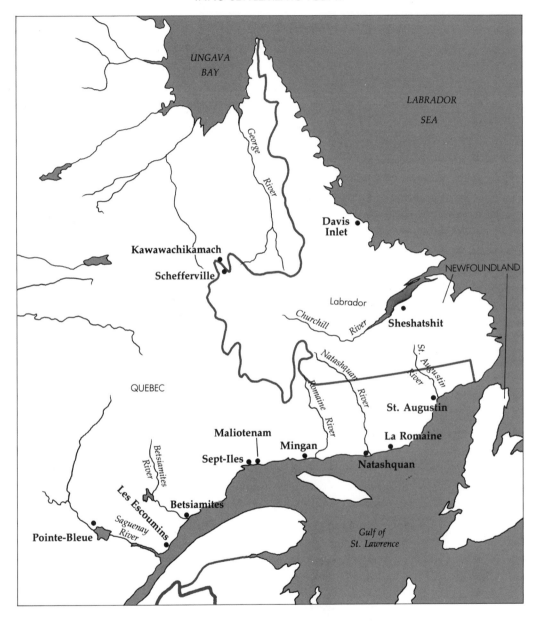

(NMIA), which was also formed in 1975 and is based in Sheshatshit. In 1976, the association sent a document to the premier of Newfoundland, Frank Moores, that requested a freeze on any further industrial development in their territory until a land-claims agreement is reached. In a later proposal, the NMIA stated, "Our rights to self-government and self-determination within the confederation of Canada must be the basis of any agreement with the Federal government. Basic to that right is the recognition of exclusive Naskapi Montagnais political jurisdiction over areas of primary importance to our life as a people." In response to this statement as well as to a report that documented historic land use by the Innu in the Quebec-Labrador peninsula, the federal government agreed to negotiate land claims with the association. However, there is no opening in the list of groups that will negotiate land claims in the near future.

There are several obstacles to the settlement of the Innu's land claims. The most serious is the Canadian government's insistence that the Indians give up rights to all of their lands in order for an agreement to be reached. Neither CAM nor the NMIA find this acceptable. Another point of contention is the Canadian government's continued efforts to proceed with industrial development, highway construction, and military flight training in Innu territory. This has greatly upset the Indians, who believe that the federal government is eliminating lands that are rightfully theirs and could otherwise be included in their land claims.

Through their negotiations, the Innu seek primarily to maintain ade-

Innu rock musicians Florent Vollant, Claude McKenzie, and Jean-Yves Fontaine performing at the "Indian Summer" festival held in Quebec in 1986. The week-long event featured documentary films, traditional food, music, craftwork, and information booths devoted to economic, political, and social issues.

The staff and students of the 1986 field session of Nutshimiun Atesseun, a program designed to develop self-reliance among unemployed persons in Innu communities.

quate lands in order to continue their hunting way of life. According to Chief Daniel Ashini, from Sheshatshit:

> We want to keep the door open to all our children and grandchildren for them to be able to pursue the traditions of our ancestors in the interior of Nitassinan. The great many Innu who continue to go into the country each fall and spring will be our lifeline to the past and to the future—a lifeline that will be of the greatest importance to us all in permitting us to pass on to future generations the great wealth of knowledge about the animals and the land that is our heritage.

The Innu also hope to establish businesses to provide employment for people who either do not wish to hunt or who wish to combine their traditional hunting activities with wage employment.

For the Innu, the current claims settlement situation is only a start. Indeed, many Innu have understandably refused to participate in negotiations until the Canadian government changes its demands. They also know that the agreements do not guarantee that their social problems will disappear. For example, the Kawawachikamach people, who signed a land-claims agreement in 1978, have not been able to eradicate depression and alcohol abuse in their community. These problems have persisted in spite of new government-funded housing, water and sewer systems, schools, and recreational facilities. The other Innu communities recognize the need to take action now in order to avoid such troubles in the future.

In this respect, the Indians have made several successful efforts to combine their traditional culture with that of mainstream Canadians. For example, in October 1986, the Attikamek-Montagnais Educational and Cultural Institute sponsored a week of cultural and informational events in Quebec City. They erected a traditional hunting camp and demonstrated traditional activities and Indian crafts. The group also presented more than 20 informational films that served to acquaint non-Indians with the native people's way of life. Innu advocacy organizations placed representatives in booths around the fairgrounds to explain contemporary Indian political issues. The fair was such a success that the participants were invited to restage it in Paris, France, during November 1986.

In the hope of revitalizing their hunting traditions, a group of Innu from Sept-Îles and Maliotenam established a series of training camps, known as Nutshimiun Atesseun. The training program, which is geared toward high school dropouts and unemployed youths, consists of three sessions—fall, winter, and spring. During the fall and spring sessions, the young people experience the routines and trials of life in an Innu hunting camp. The winter session takes place in

Sept-Îles because it is too cold for hunting. There the students learn to manufacture tools, prepare and tan hides, and become familiar with the theories behind hunting activities. The program has helped to reacquaint many Innu with their traditional heritage.

In October 1988, the Innu achieved another goal in their fight for survival as a distinct people. CAM participated in the Côte-Nord Socioeconomic Summit in Baie Comeau in which it voiced Quebec Innu concerns to representatives of the Canadian government. At the meeting, CAM delegates gained preliminary approval for the funding of 15 Innu projects, including improvement of community services and the establishment of tribal businesses.

These and other efforts on the part of the Innu have fostered a feeling of hope for the future. Their fight is nowhere near its conclusion, but the people are attempting to equip themselves with the skills they will need to deal with Canada's government and industries. The most important issue that they must face is the successful combination of the industrial life of mainstream Canada and their hunting culture. This will be difficult in a world in which their Indian values are constantly undermined. But the Innu have met such challenges successfully for many centuries. They will surely find a way to maintain their Indian identity in the future. ▲

BIBLIOGRAPHY

Bailey, Alfred Goldsworthy. *The Conflict of European and Eastern Algonkian Cultures, 1504–1700.* Toronto: University of Toronto Press, 1969.

Bonvillain, Nancy. *The Huron.* New York: Chelsea House, 1989.

Charest, Paul "Hydroelectric Dam Construction and the Foraging Activities of Eastern Quebec Montagnais." In *Politics and History in Band Societies,* edited by E. Leacock and Richard B. Lee. Cambridge, England: Cambridge University Press, 1983.

Graymont, Barbara. *The Iroquois.* New York: Chelsea House, 1988.

Henricksen, George. *Hunters in the Barrens.* St. John's, Newfoundland: Institute of Social and Economic Research, 1973.

Leacock, Eleanor. *The Montagnais "Hunting Territory" and the Fur Trade.* American Anthropological Association Memoirs (Washington, DC) 56:5 (1954), part II, pp. 1–59.

Rogers, Edward S., and Eleanor Leacock. "Montagnais-Naskapi." In *The Handbook of North American Indians,* edited by June Helm, vol. 6, pp. 169–89. Washington, DC: Smithsonian Institution, 1981.

Speck, Frank. *Naskapi.* Norman: University of Oklahoma Press, 1977.

Trigger, Bruce G. *Natives and Newcomers: Canada's "Heroic Age" Reconsidered.* Kingston and Montreal: McGill-Queen's University Press, 1985.

THE INNU AT A GLANCE

TRIBE *Innu (Montagnais-Naskapi)*

CULTURE AREA *Subarctic*

GEOGRAPHY *Mixed forest and tundra of interior and coastal portions of the eastern Quebec-Labrador peninsula*

LINGUISTIC FAMILY *Algonquian*

CURRENT POPULATION *Approximately 10,000*

FIRST CONTACT *Probably Thorvald Eriksson, Viking, 1003*

FEDERAL STATUS *Innu in Quebec are recognized as "Status Indians" under the Federal Indian Act. Innu in Labrador are as yet unrecognized by the Canadian government.*

GLOSSARY

Act for the Gradual Civilization of the Indian Tribes in the Canadas An act passed by the Canadian government in 1857 that implemented procedures designed to encourage Indians to adopt non-Indian ways and assimilate into mainstream Canadian culture.

anthropology The study of the physical, social, and historical characteristics of human beings.

archaeologist A scientist who studies past human societies through the objects, records, and settlements that people leave behind.

archaeology The recovery and reconstruction of human ways of life through the study of material culture (including tools, clothing, and food and human remains).

atanukana One of two categories of Innu myths. *Atanukana* tells of the creation of the world and of a past time during which mythical beings underwent transformations between human and animal states. See also *tipatshamuna*.

aueshish-utshimau Literally, "master of animals," the Innu word that refers to a spirit that governs a specific *tipentamuna*.

band A loosely organized group of people who are bound together by the need for food and defense, by family ties, and/or by other common interests.

bannock A type of unleavened bread eaten by Indian people.

British North America Act The 1867 act that united the Province of Canada and the British colonies of Nova Scotia and New Brunswick to create the Dominion of Canada.

caribou A type of large deer found in the arctic and subarctic regions of northern North America and Asia. In the United States, these animals are known as reindeer.

clan A multigenerational group having a shared identity, organization, and property based on belief in descent from a common ancestor. Because clan members consider themselves closely related, marriage within a clan is strictly prohibited.

Conseil Attikamek-Montagnais (CAM) An organization formed by the Quebec Innu in order to negotiate land-claims agreements with the Canadian federal and provincial governments.

culture The learned behavior of humans; nonbiological, socially taught activities; the way of life of a group of people.

dialect A regional variant of a particular language with unique elements of grammar, pronunciation, and vocabulary.

Department of Indian Affairs (DIA) A Canadian government agency that seeks to develop and implement programs that encourage Indians to manage their own affairs and to improve their educational opportunities and general social and economic well-being.

Ice Age A time in the earth's past when vast ice sheets, or glaciers, in the Arctic and Antarctic expanded to cover much of North America and Eurasia. The most recent Ice Age began about 18,000 years ago and ended about 10,000 years ago.

Indian Acts A series of acts passed by the Canadian government during the 19th century. The Indian Acts determined the nature of the political institutions that would represent Canadian Indians. These acts also made the Indians wards of the state, thus limiting their legal rights.

Jesuit A member of the Society of Jesus, a Roman Catholic order founded by Saint Ignatius Loyola in 1534. The Jesuits are highly learned and in the 17th century were particularly active in spreading Christianity outside Europe.

kamanitushit An Innu village shaman, or religious leader, who performs the *kushapatshikan* ritual.

katipenitak Literally, "controller," the Innu word used to refer to an animal spirit. See *aueshish-utshimau*.

Kuekuatsheau The mythical wolverine who the Innu believe created their world and everything in it. In the Innu's traditional stories, *Kuekuatsheau* is portrayed as an intelligent but sometimes foolish trickster.

kushapatshikan Also known as the shaking-tent ceremony, an Innu ritual performed in order to tell the future. During *kushapatshikan*, the village shaman uses a small conical tent to look into the hidden world of animal spirits and make contact with people in distant groups. According to the Innu, the shaking tent could kill those who enter it unless they had accumulated substantial spiritual power.

makushan An Innu caribou feast that often occurs around Christmastime. The ceremony, which can last as long as 12 hours, includes dancing, card playing, the ritual consumption of caribou, and other activities.

mission A religious center founded by advocates of a particular denomination who are trying to convert nonbelievers to their faith.

Naskapi Montagnais Innu Association (NMIA) An organization formed by the Labrador Innu in order to negotiate land-claims agreements with the Canadian federal and provincial governments.

nimushum Literally, "grandfather," the proper name by which a young Innu must refer to his or her male elders.

nukum Literally, "grandmother," the proper name by which a young Innu must refer to his or her female elders.

reserve, reservation A tract of land retained by Indians for their own occupation and use. *Reserve* is used to describe such lands in Canada; *reservation,* in the United States.

seigneurs During the 17th century, French merchants, religious orders, bureaucrats, and military men to whom the French crown awarded tracts of land in North America as payment for services they had performed for France.

Settlers People of mixed European and Inuit ancestry who took over much of the Innu's hunting territory during the early 20th century.

skraelings The word used in Viking epics to refer to Indian people.

Status Indians After the passage of the Indian Act of 1876, the legal designation of most of the Canadian Indians. Most Innu are now Status Indians, with the exception of those groups based in Labrador.

tipatshamuna One of two types of Innu myths. *Tipatshamuna* are historical accounts of the real-life events of Innu people, including their travels and their dealings with spirits, other peoples, and the Canadian government.

tipentamuna The Innu word for an animal kingdom. Various animal species belonged to each *tipentamuna.*

treaty A contract negotiated between representatives of the Canadian government or another national government and one or more Indian tribes. Treaties dealt with the cessation of military action, the surrender of political independence, the establishment of boundaries, terms of land sales, and related matters.

tribe A society consisting of several or many separate communities united by kinship, culture, language, and other social institutions including clans, religious organizations, and warrior societies.

utshimau The Innu word for a hunting-group leader. Usually a middle-aged man, an *utshimau* is responsible for organizing the hunt as well as lending spiritual guidance. *Utshimau* is also used to refer to an animal spirit that governs a *tipentamuna.*

Victoria Act 14 and 15 An 1851 act passed by the Canadian government that reserved 230,000 acres of land for the Indians in the southern portion of Canada.

INDEX

PICTURE CREDITS

PETER ARMITAGE is an anthropologist living in St. John's, Newfoundland. He received a B.A. in sociology and anthropology from Simon Fraser University and an M.A. from Memorial University. Since 1981, Mr. Armitage has worked among the Innu and conducted numerous research projects that examine the tribe's economy, language, religion, and land use and occupancy. He is an instructor of anthropology at Memorial University and is also research coordinator for the Naskapi Montagnais Innu Association.

FRANK W. PORTER III, general editor of INDIANS OF NORTH AMERICA, is director of the Chelsea House Foundation for American Indian Studies. He holds a B.A., M.A., and Ph.D. from the University of Maryland. He has done extensive research concerning the Indians of Maryland and Delaware and is the author of numerous articles on their history, archaeology, geography, and ethnography. He was formerly director of the Maryland Commission on Indian Affairs and American Indian Research and Resource Institute, Gettysburg, Pennsylvania, and he has received grants from the Delaware Humanities Forum, the Maryland Committee for the Humanities, the Ford Foundation, and the National Endowment for the Humanities, among others. Dr. Porter is the author of *The Bureau of Indian Affairs* in the Chelsea House KNOW YOUR GOVERNMENT series.